Eminent Indians
Revolutionaries

M.L. Ahuja

Rupa & Co

Published 2008 by

Rupa & Co

7/16, Ansari Road, Daryaganj,
New Delhi 110 002

Sales Centres:

Allahabad Bangalooru Chandigarh Chennai
Hyderabad Jaipur Kathmandu
Kolkata Mumbai

Typeset in 11.5 pts Century Schoolbook
Mindways Design
1410 Chiranjiv Tower
43 Nehru Place
New Delhi 110 019

Printed in India by
Saurabh Printers Pvt. Ltd.
A-16 Sector-IV
Noida 201 301

Revolutionaries

Other Eminent Indians titles by the author

Freedom Fighters
Scientists and Technologists
Musicians
Economists and Industrialists
Litterateurs
Film Personalities
Dancers
Legal Luminaries
Ten Great Artists
Political Thinkers and Administrators
Saints and Sages
Indian Language Litterateurs
Writings from the Raj

My parents who, though no more,
have been the source of inspiration to me

Contents

Preface   *ix*

Bhagat Singh   1

Chandra Shekhar Azad   13

Khudiram Bose   23

Ram Prasad Bismil   29

Rash Behari Bose   34

Shivaram Rajguru   41

Sukhdev Thapar   43

Mangal Pandey   45

Madan Lal Dhingra   50

Senapati Bapat   53

M.N. Roy   59

Preface

The word 'Revolutionaries' refers to the activities of a group of persons who resort to uprising against the existing authority with a view to change the administration of government, especially by violent actions. History reminds us of such uprisings which are now referred to as American Revolution (1775–8), the War of Independence carried on by the thirteen American colonies against Great Britain, Chinese Revolution (1911–12) that overthrew the authority of the Dowager Empires and the Manchu Empire which resulted in the establishment of a republic, English Revolution (1642–49) that brought about the execution of Charles I leading to the establishment of a constitutional government under William III and Mary, French Revolution (1789) that overthrew the French monarchy and culminated in the empire of Napoleon I, Russian Revolution (1917–22) that resulted in a provincial moderate government and the abdication of Nicholas II, and Indian Rebellion 1857 that culminated in India's Independence on 15 August 1947.

The Indian Rebellion of 1857 was the result of decades of ethnic and cultural differences between Indian soldiers and their British officers. The indifference of the British towards Indian rulers like the Mughals and ex-Peshwas and the annexation of Oudh were political factors that triggered dissent amongst Indians. Lord Dalhousie's policy of annexation, the doctrine of lapse, and the projected removal of the descendants of the Great Mughal from the ancestral palace to the Qutub, near Delhi, also angered some people. The specific reason that triggered the rebellion was the rumoured use of cow and pig fat in rifle cartridges. Soldiers had to break the cartridges with their teeth before loading them into their rifles. Thus, the alleged introduction of cow and pig fat offended the Hindu and Muslims alike. In February 1857, Indian soldiers in the British army refused to use their new cartridges. In March 1857, Mangal Pandey, who attacked the British sergeant and wounded an adjutant, was hanged on 7 April.

The revolt spread throughout northern India—in Meerut, Jhansi, Kanpur, Lucknow, etc. The last significant battle was fought in Gwalior on 20 June 1858 and Rani Lakshmi Bai became a martyr. Tantya Tope, the Rani of Jhansi, Kunwar Singh, the Rajput Chief of Jagadishpur in Bihar, Firuz Saha, a relative of the Mughal Emperor, Bahadur Shah and others fought with Britishers at Nasibpur, Haryana.

However, apart from a few stray incidents, the armed rebellion against the British rulers was not organised before the beginning of the 20th century. The revolutionary philosophies and movement made their presence felt during the 1905 Partition of Bengal. The initial steps to organise the revolutionaries were taken by Aurobindo Ghosh, his brother Barin Ghosh, Bhupendranath Dutta, etc. when they formed the Yugantar Party in April 1906. Yugantar was created as an inner circle of the Anushilan Samiti which was present in Bengal mainly as a revolutionary society in the guise of a fitness club. The leaders of Yugantar Party initiated steps on making explosions. Anushilan Samiti and Yugantar set up several branches throughout Bengal and other parts of India and recruited young men and women to participate in the revolutionary activities. There were several lootings and murders. Many revolutionaries were captured, imprisoned and hanged. During the First World War, the revolutionaries planned to import arms and ammunitions from Germany and stage an armed revolution against the British. The Ghadar Party operated from abroad and cooperated with the revolutionaries in India.

In the 1920s, revolutionary activists began to reorganise. Hindustan Socialist Republican Association was formed under the leadership of Chandrasekhar Azad. Bhagat Singh and Batukeshwar Dutt threw a bomb inside the Central Legislative Assembly on 8 April 1929 protesting against the passage of the Public Safety Bill and the Trade Disputes Bill. Bhagat Singh, Sukhdev and Rajguru were hanged in 1931. Thereafter, there were several raids on armouries and attempts to murder.

On 13 March 1940, Udham Singh shot Michael O'Dwyer, generally held responsible for the Amritsar massacre, in London. A number of songs composed by patriots stirred the emotions of young men and women to participate in the freedom movement, and indulge in heroic deeds as well as revolutionary activities. After the martyrdom of Bhagat Singh, a soul stirring Malayalam song rent the air:

Bhagavat Singhinte baliyude Amritasarasa kalayude paka veettum naam teerchayaai, poka poka naam!

Which means: Come, let us march forward! We will wreak vengeance for the sacrifice of Bhagat Singh, the inhuman murder at Amritsar! The Tamil film *Kappalottiya Tamizhan*, depicted the life of patriot-revolutionary, V.O. Chhidembaram Pillai and presented in it the inspiring lives of Mahakavi Bharati, Subramania Sivam Vanchinathan, all of whom dedicated their lives at the altar of the Motherland, kindled great interest to study the life of patriots and revolutionaries. Yet the immortal song, *Vande Mataram*, inspired manliness and courage in our youth to fight against dictatorship and tyranny and fostered the spirit of patriotism and respect for our hoary culture and heritage. This mantra of *Vande Mataram* propounded by Bankim Chandra Chatterjee burst like a bombshell invigorating the whole nation from Kanyakumari to Kashmir and inspired the youth to sacrifice their precious lives at the altar of the Motherland. Echoing the voice of the revolutionaries, Sri Aruobindo said, 'Liberty is the fruit we seek from the sacrifice to the Motherland the goddess to whom we offer it.'

Vande Mataram glorified the Motherland as Durga, Lakshmi and Saraswati. Every patriot from Khudiram Bose to Bhagat Singh and Rajguru died with this mantra on his lips. It became spontaneously the national anthem adopted by the mass of our people.

Let the lives of all these great patriots and revolutionaries be not cast into oblivion and let their heroic deeds be remembered by the generations to come. This indeed is the objective of this small book illustrating the deeds of some of the martyrs who sacrificed their lives to gain Independence for the succeeding generations.

In my efforts to present before you the lives and contributions of all such persons, I have consulted a number of books from various libraries, particularly that of Jamia

Milia Islamia University in New Delhi. I am grateful to the University Librarian, Dr Gyas-ud-din Makdooni and his staff members for giving me access to the books. I would like to thank Rupa & Co for undertaking publication of the series of books on Eminent Indians. The current book is only one part. My wife, Mrs Asha Ahuja, also deserves my thanks for cooperating with me in my efforts to concentrate on this project. I also received continued encouragement from Mr Saurabh Bhagat, Dr Rahul Malhotra, Mrs Lovelina Bhagat and Dr Chetna Malhotra among my family members. My thanks are due to them. My thanks are also due to various other people who helped me in one way or the other in my endeavours.

31 January 2008   **M.L. Ahuja**
New Delhi

Bhagat Singh

Bhagat Singh was a romantic revolutionary whose endeavours culminated in India's Independence from the British colonial rule in 1947. He was one of those young patriots whose extreme sacrifice made him a heroic symbol idolised by thousands of youth in the country. He appeared like a meteor in the political sky for a brief period and became a cynosure of millions of eyes as well as the symbol of the spirit and aspirations of new India. Bhagat Singh's energetic youthful charisma proved a potential challenge to the British Raj and the popularity he achieved consequently is amazing. He was dauntless in the face of death, determined to smash imperialist rule and raise on its ruins the edifice of free India. His sense of virility, style, simple lifestyle, writings, statements, speeches and acts of defiance against the British Raj transformed the story of his short career unequivocally into a colourful legend. His innate feelings, woven into the following song have made him immortal.

Kabhi who din bhi ayega, ke jab azad ham hongey,
Yeh apni zameen hogi, yeh apna asmaan hoga,
Shaheedon ki chitaon par, lagengey har baar mele,
Watan par marney walon ka, yeh hi baki nishaan
hoga.

Which means: A day will come when we shall be free; this will be our own earth and this will be our own sky; fairs will be held in celebration where patriots are martyred. It will be a fitting monument for those who die for the nation.

These, in fact, were the words of a revolutionary, Om Prakash, recited by Bhagat Singh when he appeared before the Tribunal on 5 May 1930 in the Assembly Bomb Blast case. It enraged Justice Coldstream who was presiding over the case. The slogan of *Inquilab Zindabad* (long live the revolution) reverberated through the hall. Bhagat Singh wanted to infuse revolutionary ideals and tactics in the public through such catchy slogans. Consequently, the proceedings were suspended. Undaunted by the Britishers' hard punishment, Bhagat Singh found contentment only in Ram Prasad Bismal's song, which he kept humming till his last moment.

> *Mera rang de basanti chola,*
> *Issi rang mein rang ke Shiva nein,*
> *Maan ka bandhan khola,*
> *Mera rang de basanti chola,*
> *Yeh hi rang haldi ghaati mein,*
> *Khul karke tha khela,*
> *Nav basant mein Bharat ke hi,*
> *Veeron ka yeh mela,*
> *Mera rang de basanti chola.*

Bhagat Singh was named Bhaganwala at birth by his family members. After becoming the country's hero and going to the gallows, he was referred to as Shaheed Bhagat Singh. He was indeed a *bhagat*—a saint or devotee of Mother India—in the true sense. The statue of Bhagat

Singh unveiled on 23 March 1973 by Prime Minister Indira Gandhi in Bhagat Singh's hometown continues to echo his words imploring his mother to prepare a *basanti chola* (the yellow robe). This is the colour, which the revolutionaries put on before going to the gallows. For Bhagat Singh, *basant* or spring symbolized freedom. The yellow of spring betokened for him sacrifice. He knew it fully well that sacrifice was the key to country's Independence.

Born on 27 September 1907 in Banga in Punjab State of northern India, Bhagat Singh was the son of Kishan Singh and Vidyawati. He was born in a family with glorious revolutionary traditions. His grandfather was the first to set the ball rolling by showing inclination towards Arya Samaj after meeting Swami Dayanand, even though he was a Jat Sikh. His grandfather, Arjun Singh's involvement with Arya Samaj only shows that he was ready to receive new ideas. He got his sons, Kishan Singh and Ajit Singh, admitted to the Saindas Anglo-Sanskrit School. Bhagat Singh's father was also involved in revolutionary activities. The day Bhagat Singh was born his father was released on bail from the Central Jail in Lahore and the order for the release of his elder uncle, Ajit Singh, who was in prison in Mandalay, was also released on that day. His younger uncle, Swaran Singh, was simultaneously released from the Lahore Central Jail. All these strange coincidences held great joy for the family which decided to name the child 'Bhagwanwala', who heralded luck to the family.

Bhagat Singh's father, Kishan Singh, and his uncle, Ajit Singh, were Amritdhari sikhs. They were inspired by Guru Gobind Singh's great sacrifices. Their love for the motherland and obsession to ensure its emancipation from the British rule turned them revolutionaries and face incarceration. The social and political consciousness in Punjab, which had earlier begun with Guru Nanak and was consolidated as a sense of nationalism with the coming of Guru Nanak gradually spread to other parts of the country. The Akali wave in Punjab, the Arya Samaj movement, the struggle of the Indian National Congress, the Kirti Kisan movement were vital ingredients of reformism and militancy.

Bhagat Singh's forefathers belonged to a small village, known as Khatkharkalan in the Doab in northern India. This village had become the centre of the freedom movement. Ajit Singh's wife, Harnam Kaur—Bhagat Singh's aunt—would take the boy in her lap and recount to him the exploits and adventures of Ajit Singh. This had a profound effect on the young mind. In this situation, young Bhagat Singh was obviously obsessed with the spirit of the freedom movement right from his days in the cradle. He had listened to the agony and torture inflicted by the Britishers on his forefathers and he nursed the spirit of revenge in his mind. The boy was just two-year old when mango saplings were being planted on Kishan Singh's land. He broke some twigs and began to plant them in the ground. Anand Kishore remarked to Bhagat Singh's father, 'Your son is already a farmer, and is planting trees,' at which Kishan Singh asked Bhagat, 'What are you up to, son?' Bhagat Singh replied calmly, 'Father, I am planting guns!'

Right from his childhood, Bhagat Singh seemed to have prepared himself to meet British violence with violence. The boy had a streak of seriousness in his temperament. When he was in the fourth class, he had already read books by his uncle Ajit Singh, Sufi Amba Prasad and Lala Hardyal. Literature on the world's revolutionary movements was available to him in his home. From childhood itself, he enjoyed the company of revolutionaries like Mehta Anand Kishore, Lala Pindi Das and Sufi Amba Prasad. Under the influence of all that he heard from them, he had turned on to the path of the freedom struggle. He was greatly influenced by Koma Gata Maru. The spirit of sacrifices that his uncle, Ajit singh, embodied was always uppermost in his mind. The hanging of his nineteen-year old friend, Kartar Singh, in the Lahore Conspiracy Case had a profound effect on the nine-year old Bhagat Singh. He always carried Kartar's photograph. A verse that Kartar used to sing always reverberated in his mind was:

Seva desh di jindarhiye barhi aukhi
Gallan karniandher sukhalian ne
Jinan desh seva vich paer paya
Onan lakh museebatan jhalian ne

Which means: It is easy to talk but difficult to serve the country. Those who have ventured into serving the nation have had to pass through pain and misery.

In 1917, when his office transferred Bhagat Singh's father to Lahore, the boy joined D.A.V. Middle School. When the tragic Jallianwala Bagh incident took place on 13 April 1919, Bhagat Singh reached Amritsar and made obeisance to the blood-drenched earth and brought with him some earth to Lahore put in a jar. He swore to avenge with blood this shedding of blood. In August 1921, when Mahatma Gandhi began his non-cooperation movement, Bhagat Singh left school while in ninth class and joined the non-cooperation movement. But after some time he joined the National College in Lahore. Bhai Parmanand and Lala Lajpat Rai established this college for those who had left their institutions to join the non-cooperation movement. In this college, he was impressed with his history professor, Vidya Alankar. He studied seriously the history of revolutionaries and social movements of the world. He participated and acted as hero in two plays.

In 1924, when Bhagat Singh's mother was planning his marriage, he left home and arrived in Kanpur to join the revolutionary activities. There he met Ganesh Shankar Vidyarthi. He joined the Pratap Press and changed his name to Balwant Singh. In his leisure time, Bhagat Singh read the history of revolutions in different countries and about communism. He became a member of the Hindustan Republican Association. As a member of the Association, he went to villages in Uttar Pradesh to distribute books and leaflets about revolutionaries. The young men in schools and colleges, workers and peasants were educated on violent revolution. Ganesh Shankar Vidyarthi was impressed with Bhagat Singh's courage and capacity for revolutionary work. It was through Vidyarthi's influence that Bhagat Singh was appointed Headmaster in National School of Shadipur in Aligarh district in northern India. There he instilled in the students a love for the nation and encouraged them to work for its independence.

Six months had elapsed since Bhagat Singh left Lahore. His family had no inkling of his whereabouts. His grandmother became very ill. In 1924, he returned to Lahore but in 1925 he had to leave for Kanpur in connection with the Kakori Dacoity Case to help members of the Hindustan Socialist Association to escape from jail.

With the help of Vidya Alankar, Bhagat Singh was able to get a job in a newspaper, *Vir Arjun*, where he worked for about six months, assuming the name of Balwant Singh.

In 1919, a Commission under the chairmanship of Sir John Simon was set up to introduce administrative reforms, but Indian leaders were not happy because of the non-inclusion of Indian leaders in it. This further precipitated militant activities under Bhagat Singh. On 30 October 1928, a large rally was organised against the members of the Commission. Lala Lajpat Rai and Bhagat Singh led the procession. A large number of people were injured in the *lathi*-charge. Lala Lajpat Rai was seriously injured and then expired. Bhagat Singh had witnessed the barbarous act of the Superintendent of Police, Scott. It stirred his sentiments further. The death of Lala Lajpat Rai was a great loss to Bhagat Singh who itched to answer British violence with violence. Sukh Dev, Raj Guru, Chander Shekhar Azad and Jai Gopal joined him.

Bhagat Singh and Sukh Dev slipped from Lahore to Amritsar. Here they met some revolutionaries and set up a bomb-making factory in Agra with branches in Lahore and Saharanpur. They decided to throw bombs in the Assembly when the Public Safety Bill and the Trader Disputes Bill were presented. After throwing the bombs Bhagat Singh and B.K. Dutt stood still. There was no fear on their faces. They were arrested and they confessed having thrown the bombs. In a statement made by them jointly before the court of the session judge they stated: 'The bomb was necessary to awaken England from her dreams.' They said that they were inspired by the ideals, which guided Guru Gobind Singh and Shivaji and held human life sacred beyond words. When asked in the lower court what he meant by revolution, Bhagat Singh replied: 'Revolution doesn't necessarily involve sanguinary strife nor is there any place in it for individual vendetta. By revolution we mean that the present order of things, which is based on manifest injustice, must change. By revolution we mean the ultimate establishment of an order of society.... At the altar of this revolution, we have brought our youth as an incense, for no sacrifice is too great for so magnificent a cause.'

The session judge dismissed the statement of Bhagat Singh and B.K.Dutt. Both were sentenced to transportation for life and they appealed to the High Court. But the High Court endorsed the decision of the session judge on 13 January 1930. While in jail, Bhagat Singh met the old revolutionaries of the Ghadar Movement. He saw that the political prisoners were being badly treated. He, therefore, launched jails reform movement and organised hunger strike. He claimed some facilities for the political prisoners. The authority was forced to yield and a Jail Inquiry Committee was constituted. When the Committee recommended a number of facilities, they ended their strike.

In his teenage years, Bhagat Singh became a member of an organisation, Naujawan Bharat Sabha (Youth Society of India). In this Sabha, Bhagat Singh and his fellow revolutionaries grew popular amongst the youth. He also joined the Hindustan Republication Association at the request of Professor Vidyalankar, which was then headed by Ram Prasad Bismil and Ashfaqulla Khan. He wrote for and edited Urdu and Punjabi newspapers published from Amritsar. His political thought evolved gradually from Gandhian nationalism to revolutionary Marxism. By the end of 1928, he and his comrades renamed their organisation the Hindustan Socialist Republican Association. He had read the teachings of Karl Marx, Friedrich Engels and Vladimir Lenin and believed that with such a large and diverse population, India could only survive properly under a socialist regime. These ideals had been introduced to him during his time at the National College at Lahore and he believed that India should re-enact the Russian Revolution. This and his militant methods put him at odds with Mahatma Gandhi and members of the Congress.

On 10 July 1929, the Lahore Conspiracy case came up for hearing before a special magistrate in the jail itself. When Bhagat Singh reached the court, slogans like *Inquilab Zindabad* electrified the atmosphere. He started by reciting a poem of the revolutionary Om Prakash: '*Kabhi who din bhi aye ga, ke jab azad ham hongey...*' The proceedings of the Tribunal had to be suspended. When the hearing was resumed the same drama was repeated. Bhagat Singh and his comrades were charged with 'a conspiracy and war against the King Emperor by murder, dacoity and other methods, including the manufacture and use of bombs.' Bhagat Singh was not prepared to defend himself. His father sent a representation to the Viceroy through the Tribunal. But Bhagat Singh was unhappy and wrote to his father: 'My life is not precious—at least to me—as you probably think it to be. It is not at all worth buying at the cost of my principles.'

The Tribunal found Bhagat Singh guilty in the Lahore Conspiracy Case and sentenced him to be 'hanged by the neck till he is dead' along with Sukh Dev Singh and Raj Guru. Bhagat Singh sacrificed his family attachments for his ideals. For him, love of humanity subordinated love for parents and other close relatives. Independence for mankind was an article of faith with him. For embracing this ideal he was moving steadily and fearlessly to the gallows. The moment he was anxiously waiting for came at last. He was full of joy. The thought of parting with their son for ever sent his parents to despair. Their minds were in agony. The time of their son's execution was announced. But Bhagat Singh was happy as his actions were being recorded in red-letter words. The season of spring and its outbreak created joy in his mind. He yearned to see it in a changing context. In the last days, his mind sought contentment in only one thing—the words of a song by Ram Prashad Bismal, which he kept humming all the time: '*Mera rang dey basanti chola, Issi rang mein rang ke Shiv nen maan ka bandhan khola....*'

Bhagat Singh did not appeal for mercy. On the contrary, he appealed for being executed by shooting. He asked the jail authorities that he and his comrades should be treated as political prisoners and not as criminals. He refused to be handcuffed and to be dressed in black apparel. Addressing the Deputy Commissioner of Lahore, Bhagat Singh remarked: 'Well, Mr. Magistrate, you are fortunate to be able today to see how Indian revolutionaries can embrace death with pleasure for the sake of their supreme ideal.' After saying this, Bhagat Singh, Sukh Dev and Raj Guru moved forward to the hangman's platform. They were shouting slogans like 'Long Live the Revolution and Down with British Imperialism' as they moved. Each of them put his neck in the noose and said to the hangman: 'Please arrange the rope!' In a few minutes, their soul left their bodies. In the darkness of the night, the bodies were taken to a village Gandasingwala in district Ferozepur. They were incompletely cremated on the shore of the Sutlej and their bodies were thrown into the river.

Bhagat Singh was fond of reading books. He is believed to have devoted his time in jail to creative writings. In the condemned cell, he kept reading books on socialism. Among the books, which he wrote, while in incarceration, are stated to be: *Militarism, Why Men Fight, Leftwing Communism, Mutual Aid, Field, Factory and Worship, Civil War in France, Land Revolution in Russia, Theory of Historical Materialism*, and, *Door to Death, Autobiography, The Revoluitionary Movement of India* with biographic sketches of the revolutionaries. Some people say that he sent the manuscripts out of jail through his younger brother who handed them over to a lady for publication. Somehow, they have never been published.

Bhagat Singh is no more. But the ecstatic feelings that he experienced in kindling the flame of freedom in India and his martyrdom is epitomised in his following words:

Sarfarozi ki tamanna ab hamare dil mein hae
Dekhna hai zor kitna bauzzu-e-qaatal mein hae

Which means: The desire to lay down our lives has grown in our hearts. Now, we have to test how much strength resides in the arms of the killer.

His extreme patriotism led him almost to worship freedom. His worship took the form of violence and weapons. Bhagat Singh's energetic youthful charisma proved a potential challenge to the British Raj and the popularity he achieved is amazing. He was dauntless in the face of death, determined to smash imperialist rule and raise on its ruins the edifice of free India. He had full trust in the fortitude and patience that characterised the Sikh movement. Progressive Sikh ideology, the philosophy of revolution fought by Marx, Engels and Lenin, the socialist ideas of Mazzini and Garibaldi—these were the pillars of Bhagat Singh's socialism. A fluent orator, amiable and considerate to others, he was obsessed with nation's agony over the heinous crime of hurling *lathi* blows at Lala Lajpat Rai. His selfless sacrifice for the cause of the Motherland will continue to instill the feelings of patriotism in the generations to come.

Chandra Shekhar Azad

Chandra Shekhar Azad, often called Panditji since he was a devout Brahmin, was the founder of the Garam Dal. He was one of the pioneers of the revolutionary struggle with arms against the oppressive Britishers. Azad believed it to be his *dharma* to fight for his fellow Indians. According to him, a soldier never relinquished his weapon. Rightly so, he died with his weapon in his hand, fighting the British and became a martyr at the tender age of twenty-four. Along with revolutionaries like Bhagat Singh, Rajguru, Sukhdev, Bhagwati Charan, Saligram Shukla, Batukeshwar Dutt, Bejoy Kumar Sinha, Siya Verma and Sadashiv Rao, he spearheaded the freedom movement. A born leader, he was determined not to die of a British bullet or be captured and hanged. In his lifetime, Azad managed to keep both his pledges.

Chandra Shekhar Azad was born on 23 July 1906 in a bamboo hut plastered with mud in Bhavra village, Madhya Pradesh. He was the son of a watchman in the royal gardens, Pandit Sitaram Tiwari and Jagarani Devi. Sitaram was originally a native of Badarka in Unnao district of modern Uttar Pradesh. However, he had to leave his ancestral house in search of livelihood and finally settled in Bhav.

It was here that Chandra Shekhar spent his early days as a child among the Bhil boys. Once while celebrating Diwali with some tribal children, he held the entire matchbox on his right palm and burnt them in a flash. The matchsticks caught fire but he continued to hold them on his palm till all of them were burnt emitting different kinds of colours. Thereafter, he told his tribal friends: 'Look, this is how you should learn to bear the pain.'

Chandra Shekhar received his primary education in the local village school. For higher studies, he went to the Sanskrit Pathashala at Varanasi. But more than the books, he was interested in running along brooks, climbing trees, and playing with cattle. He was also adept in wrestling, archery and mock fighting. In Varanasi, he learnt Sanskrit and studied the *Shastras* (scriptures). When the non-violent non-cooperation movement was withdrawn, his mind became restless and he was drawn towards the revolutionary movement. Benares, at that time, was the stronghold of the movement. Soon he came in contact with Manmath Nath Gupta and Pranvesh Chatterji, and became a member of the Hindustan Prajatantra Sangh (Hindustan Republican Association). He was an ardent follower of Lord Hanuman and once even disguised himself as priest in a Hanuman temple to escape the dragnet of British police.

The Jallianwala Bagh massacre in Amritsar in 1919 deeply troubled Chandra Shekhar. Meanwhile in recognition of his leadership qualities, he was elected the Commander-in-Chief of the armed wing of the Republican Association. Subsequently, at the tender age of fourteen, he was arrested by the police for taking part in the non-cooperation movement. When the British magistrate asked his name, his father's name and his residential address, he, while a student of Benares Sanskrit Pathshala, replied that his name was *Azad* (independent), his father's name was *Swatantra* (independence) and his residence was prison. The magistrate was red with rage and ordered him to be flogged for the impertinent reply. A special whip was brought for him and Chandra Shekhar was stripped to the skin. His body was then fastened to the flogging triangle. It was a public flogging, which the Britishers had introduced during the Jallianwalla Bagh massacre. With every new lash the boy-rebel shouted: *Vande Mataram, Mahatma Gandhi Ki Jai, Bharat Mata ki Jai.* Even when his skin was torn and he was bleeding profusely he continued shouting slogans of freedom and in praise of his Motherland. His endurance stunned his captor. At the end of the fifteenth cane lash, three *annas* (fraction of a rupee, the then Indian currency) were placed on the boy's palm according to the rules of the prison. But the boy had the audacity to throw away the three coins on the jailor's face and stood defiant like a wounded lion. Through his act of defiance, he endeared himself to the masses which raised him on their shoulders, took out a procession and felicitated him at Gyanvapi locality in Benares. It was here that he was first hailed as 'Azad'. Since then he came to be known as Chandra Shekhar Azad.

In 1924, Azad was made the head of the U.P unit. Within a short span, he became a terror to the British police and the people started referring to him as 'a hero of the hundred fights'. The party to which he was associated was renamed as Hindustan Samajwadi Prajatantra Sangh (The Hindustan Socialist Republican Association), an organisation which stood for the freedom of India through armed revolution. They aimed to establish a socialist state based on secularism, with a prominent role for women.

In October 1924, an All India Conference of Revolutionaries was held at Kanpur and leaders from different parts of India attended it. The British Government called it a 'terrorist organisation' and attributed the tag of the 'most persistent terrorist organisation outside Bengal'. It was subsequently styled as the 'Hindustan Socialist Republican Association'. Two Bengalis originally started it after the failure of Mahatma Gandhi's first mass civil disobedience campaign in UP with the object of establishing a Federal system of governance on the lines of the United States through an organised and armed revolution. Collection of money and arms was made mandatory. To achieve this, in some cases, it was deemed proper to even resort to assassination. In all such armed actions, Azad was in the forefront.

The first armed action towards this end in view was the Kakori train hold-up case, which took place on 9 August 1925. The plot was devised by Azad with the help of Ram Prasad Bismil of 'Sarfaroshi' song fame. In this case, ten young men boarded the train at Kakori railway station, which was proceeding towards Alamnagar in Saharanpur-Lucknow sector, and seized the government treasury. The British Government called it 'robbery' but the freedom fighters termed it as 'national service'. The British police somehow came to know of the plot. As a result, Ram Prasad Bismil, Ashfaqullah Khan, Roshan Singh and Lahiri were arrested and later hanged. But Chandra Shekhar remained elusive and couldn't be arrested.

After this incident, Azad shifted to Jhansi. There he lived in one room provided to him by his employer, Bundelkhand Motor Company. He worked there as a mechanic under the assumed name of Hari Shankar, while continuing his activities as a revolutionary. He even drove the Police Superintendant's car. He often chatted with the police officials in the Jhansi Police Station, but nobody even suspected that such a simple person could be a revolutionary. One of his neighbours, Ram Dayal, often got drunk at night and beat his wife which disturbed the colony's peace. One day, Chandra Shekhar asked Ram Dayal to stop beating his wife. Ram Dayal abused Chandra Shekhar, calling him '*saala*' (brother-in-law). 'Now, if you beat her I am bound to save my sister,' said Chandra Shekhar. In a drunken state, Ram Dayal beat his wife again, dragged her from her hair and raised his hand indicating his resolve to beat her again. Chandra Shekhar couldn't tolerate the injustice being perpetrated against the woman. He held Ram Dayal's hand and jerked him away. He then thrashed him with his fist thrice till Dayal came to his senses. Dayal now fell at Chandra Shekhar's feet and pledged not to beat his wife again. Chandra Shekhar could never stand wrong done to others and possessed the strength and stamina of an epic hero.

Once, Chandra Shekhar came across a Pathan thrashing a labourer who had not paid back his loan in time. Chandra Shekhar intervened and said: 'Khan Baba, give him some time and he will pay your money back.' But the Khan didn't like the intervention and warned Chandra Shekhar to keep away else he too would have to bear the brunt of his wrath. At this, Chandra Shekhar pounced upon the money lending Pathan, forcing him to flee and never to return. After this incident, the children of the locality started calling Azad as 'Lion'. Thereafter, people began looking up to him for help. The police in Jhansi got suspicious. When Azad found that the police had come to know of the reality, he slipped off to Orchha, constructed a hut on the banks of a river and started living there.

By this time, the Hindustan Socialist Republican Association decided to hold a black flag demonstration at Lahore on 30 October 1928 to protest against the visit of Simon Commission, which didn't include a single Indian. Azad joined this demonstration. Punjab Kesri Lala Lajpat Rai, Bhagat Singh, Chandra Shekhar and many other revolutionaries led this peaceful demonstration. The British police, for whom Lala Lajpat Rai had become an eyesore, pounced on him without any provocation. Though Lala Lajpat Rai looked frail but his spirit was dauntless. *Lathis* (canes) were hurled on him but he stood like a rock, not permitting his people to hit back. The people, who witnessed such atrocities, wondered how Lalaji could withstand the blows without collapsing on the spot. The Superintendent of Police, Mr Scott, personally conducted the operation in Lahore. Bhagat Singh could not control his emotions and wanted to retaliate, but Lala Lajpat Rai stopped him. In the evening, Lala Lajpat Rai roared: 'Every blow that they hurled at us will drive a nail in the coffin of the British empire.' This prophecy ultimately came true. The sixty-three year old Lala Lajpat Rai died in Lahore hospital eighteen days after this incident, i.e. on 17 November 1928. But his words haunted Azad and reminded him of his obligation to retaliate.

The Hindustan Socialist Republican Association attributed this as a national humiliation. Meetings were held every night and it was decided to avenge the death of Lala Lajpat Rai. Chander Shekhar masterminded the plot to kill Scott on the night of 17 December though the task was assigned to Bhagat Singh. Bhagat Singh and

Rajguru besieged the office of the police superintendent. As soon as a white man in police uniform came out of the office of the police superintendent and started driving his motor cycle, Rajguru fired the first shot which hit the officer who turned out to be J.P. Saunders, Assistant Superintendent of Police instead of Scott, the Superintendent. The bullet hit Saunders on his forehead and he fell down from his motor cycle. Bhagat Singh moved ahead and fired four more shots and Saunders died instantly. When the bodyguard chased Bhagat Singh and Rajguru, Azad killed the bodyguard with a single shot. Next day, people saw posters throughout Lahore announcing that Lala Lajpat Rai's death had been avenged.

Subsequently, Bhagat Singh and Rajguru sought shelter in a house. Azad got asylum in a house, which belonged to a freedom fighter's widow. The woman was too worried about the marriage of his daughter but had no money. The police had announced a reward of Rs 10,000 to the informer of Chandra Shekhar Azad. Seeing the plight of the woman Azad pleaded to the woman: '*Bhabhi*, inform the police, get this money and arrange the marriage.' The lady got enraged and reprimanded Azad for his 'foolish' offer saying, 'My daughter will remain unmarried but I cannot bear the stigma of being a traitor. I'm a freedom fighter's widow and I will hold aloft the flag of freedom.'

It is said that Chandra Shekhar Azad slipped away at night. While leaving, he placed a bundle of ten thousand rupees on the table and headed towards another house of Durga Bhabhi. He then decided to go to Calcutta (now, Kolkata). Incidentally, Azad happened to travel along with a Sadhu singing *bhajans* (devotional songs) while Rajguru sat in the servant's coupe, which was attached to the first class where Bhagat Singh was attired as a 'Sahib' and Durga Bhabhi as Sahib's wife. In such an ingenuous disguise, the British Government failed to detect them.

Chandra Shekhar Azad was given the responsibility of planning a plot to throw a live bomb in the Central Assembly at Delhi. The job was allotted to Bhagat Singh and Batukeshwar Dutt. On 8 April 1929, two bombs were thrown in such a manner that no one was killed or injured. Only four members were hurt slightly and that too as a result of the commotion caused. A red pamphlet was also thrown on the floor of the House, where the purpose of throwing the bomb was made clear. It was not to kill anyone. Its purpose was only to awaken the administration. After this incident, Bhagat Singh and Dutt volunteered arrest while Azad escaped.

In his next move, Chandra Shekhar Azad resolved to blow up the train by which the Viceroy was travelling. The duty was assigned to Yash Pal in December 1929. The explosion took place near Purana Qila railway track in Delhi but the Viceroy had a providential escape. The special train however was damaged. On 6 July 1930, Azad masterminded an armed robbery, looting a Delhi firm of Rs 14,000. With most of his comrades, either in prison or dead, he was left alone to fight the British empire. To hoodwink the British police, at times, he worked in Punjab as a motor-driver, a cook, a boatman or a mechanic. He even planned to free Bhagat Singh from the Lahore central jail on the day he was to be taken to the court. But the government decided to have the military court inside the jail.

In February 1931, Chandra Shekhar Azad held discussions in Alfred Park, Allahabad. He planned a mass revolution on the lines of Bolshevik Revolution in Russia. On 27 February 1931, the police came to know that Azad was having a meeting with his associate Sukhdev Raj. The Police Superintendent fired at Azad, which hit his thigh. He remained conscious and hid himself behind a tree. From there, he fired back. The bullet injured the Police Superintendent's wrist. When the CID Inspector came to the SP's rescue, Azad broke his jaw and fought like a lion when the other policemen surrounded him. The police rained bullets on him from all sides. A bullet penetrated into his leg but he got up, took his position and fired back. With three bullets he injured three police officers. Another bullet from the police injured Azad's left arm but he still kept fighting. His body was riddled with bullets but he continued fighting. When only one bullet was left with him, he placed the gun against his temple, fired his last shot and fell dead. Four bullets and a part of fifth were extracted from his body as per post-mortem report. He was cremated at Rasulabad Ghat under heavy police security.

Chandra Shekhar Azad is no more but he endeared himself to future generations as a great freedom fighter and a revolutionary with an indomitable will power. He never tolerated injustice towards human beings and was always ready to help needy people. In this way, he has carved out a distinct place for himself in Indian history, especially in the Indian freedom movement. Azad is a hero to many Indians today. Alfred Park was renamed Chandrasekhar Azad Park, as have been scores of schools, colleges, roads and other public institutions across India. Ever since Manoj Kumar's film, *Shaheed Bhagat Singh* was released in 1964, Azad's character has become central to any film or commemoration of the life of Bhagat Singh. In the film, *The Legend of Bhagat Singh*, starring Ajay Devgan, Azad (played by Akhilendra Mishra) had a prominent role and was shown to kill himself rather than dying at the hands of foreigners. The patriotism of Azad, Sukhdev, Bismil and Ashfaqulla Khan was also depicted in *Rang De Basanti*, a contemporary Bollywood film starring Aamir Khan that was released in February 2006. His contribution to India's freedom struggle has truly made him immortal and he continues to live in the hearts of Indians as an unparalleled revolutionary.

Khudiram Bose

It was February 1906. A grand exhibition had been arranged at Medinipur in Bengal. The intention was to hide the injustice of the British then ruling India. On exhibition were articles like pictures and puppets to create the impression that the British rulers, though foreigners, were doing much to help the state of the people of India. There was a huge crowd to see the exhibition.

'Take care, don't touch my body', said a young man, who appeared with a bundle of handbills. He was distributing them to the people. The handbill bore the title, *Sonar Bangla* and carried the slogan *Vande Mataram*. In addition, he exposed the true purpose of the British in putting up the exhibition. He also explained the various forms of British injustice and tyranny.

The boy was soon noticed by a policeman present there who pulled at his bundle of handbills. But to catch the boy was not so easy. He jerked his hand free, swung his arm and powerfully struck the nose of the policeman. Again, he took possession of the handbills and shouted, 'Take care, don't touch my body! I will see how you arrest me without a warrant.' Saying this he disappeared immediately. Later, a case was filed against the boy but the court set him free on account of his tender age. The heroic boy who distributed handbills so bravely at the Medinipur exhibition and thus defeated the purpose of the British was the martyr Khudiram Bose.

Khudiram was born on 3 December 1889 in the village Mohobony in Medinipur district, West Bengal. He was the son of Trilokyanath Basu and Lakshmipriya Devi. Trailokyanath Basu was a Tehsildar of the town of the Nadazol prince. His mother Lakshmipriya Devi was a pious lady who was well known for her virtuous life and generousity. Though a few children were born to the couple, all died soon after birth. Only a daughter survived of the lot. The Bose couple yearned for a male child. Khudiram was their last child. They however did not live long enough to enjoy their happiness and died unexpectedly when Khudiram was just six. Consequently, the boy's elder sister, Anurupadevi and his brother-in-law Amritalal had to shoulder the responsibility of bringing him up.

Anurupadevi looked after Khudiram with the affection of a mother. She wanted her younger brother to be highly educated, get a high post and make a name for himself. She, therefore, got him admitted to a nearby school. Khudiram was a smart boy and could grasp things easily. But he was not attentive in class. A patriot, even at the age of seven, Khudiram used to think, 'India is our country. It is a great country. Elders say that this has been the home of knowledge for thousands of years. Why then are the red-faced British here? Under them, our people cannot even live as they wish. When I grow up, I must somehow drive them out.' Throughout the day the boy was engaged in these thoughts and his anguish grew day by day.

Once Khudiram went to a temple. There he saw a few people lying on the bare ground in front of the temple.

'Why are these people lying thus?' he asked the people present there. He was told that they were suffering from some disease and had made a vow to be there without food and water. They would get up only after God appeared in their dream and promised to cure their diseases. This incident really struck Khudiram hard and he decided that one day he too would give up all thought of hunger and thirst and would lie on the ground like those people. According to him, there could not be a disease worse than slavery and he was poised to end it.

As a child, Khudiram was influenced by the notion of *karma* in *Bhagavad Gita*. He received his early education in Hamilton School, Tamlook. Like any other boy of his age, he was interested in reading detective novels and loved to play the flute. During his school days, Khudiram was inspired by activists like Satyendranath and Gyanendranath Bose, who headed a secret society to campaign and fight against the British supremacy. He played the role of a saviour when Kangsabati got flooded, saving a number of lives. When Lord Curzon partitioned Bengal on 16 October 1905, Khudiram was a young man of seventeen. He was witness to the uproar and conflagration that followed, and saw the radicals swearing their blood for the cause of freedom. Aroused by the call, he joined *Yugantar,* the secret outfit created by Aurobindo Ghosh, Barin Ghosh and Raja Subodh Malik. He felt disillusioned with the British following the partition of Bengal.

In February 1906, Khudiram ran an errand for the Medinipur-based outfit of the extremists. He became a household name in those parts of Bengal after hitting a police officer and escaping after being arrested at the grounds of Medinipur old jail for distributing a nationalist propaganda called *Sonar Bangla*. He also robbed mailbags to accumulate funds for the society's operations.

Khudiram seemed to have inherited the love for his motherland with his mother's milk. Although he lost his mother when just a child, her image and affection remained indelible in his unconscious mind. He was greatly influenced by Bankim Chandra's song, *Bande Mataram*. Rani Lakshmi Bai, Veer Kunwar Singh of Bihar and Bahadur Shah Zafar were among the leading lights of the First War of Indian Independence in 1857. Bankim Chandra Chatterjee was then a young man of seventeen who saw with great pain how Indians, though heroic and intelligent, were defeated due to the lack of discipline, organisation, and paucity of arms and ammunition. Also, a number of Indians turned out to be traitors, self-seekers and opportunists. Bankim in his novel, *Anandamath*, described the fight of the patriotic ascetics (*sanyasis*) against foreign rule. His intention was to awaken patriotism among the people and inspire them to fight for freedom. The freedom fighting *sanyasis* in the novel sing *Vande Mataram* as a song of inspiration. Within a few days of the publication of the novel, the song became a favourite mantra of patriots like Khudiram who learnt the use of weapons like the pistol, the dagger and the *lathi* as an inspiration from the novel. Khudiram also took up the task of spreading the gospel of *Vande Mataram*. In his mind, he visualised the image of Bharat Mata in all her splendour and started explaining the meaning of *Vande Mataram* to his friends. He also encouraged them to read the novel *Anandamath*. After reading Bankim Chandra's novel, *Anandamath*, he was so influenced that he not only organised the freedom movement but also became a martyr himself.

The immediate provocation for the revolutionaries was the partition of Bengal by the British with a view to split Hindus and the Muslims. In the western part of Bengal, the Hindus were in majority while in the eastern part it was the Muslims. Thousands of Indians rebelled against the British. Khudiram was greatly influenced by this movement. The cry of *Vande Mataram* caught his imagination. He watched with interest the different forms of protest against the partition of Bengal.

By this time, the Chief Presidency Magistrate Kingsford had gained notoriety by passing out stiff sentences against the nationalist activists. He ordered to cane a youth called Sushil Sen for contempt of the court. Sushil was left nearly dead and the incident caused a furore throughout Bengal. The *Yugantar* passed Kingsfosrd's death sentence and Khudiram and Prafulla Chaki were chosen for the job. At the nascent age of sixteen, Khudiram defied the police after planting bombs near police stations and targeting government officials. He was arrested three years later on charges of conducting a series of bomb attacks. The specific bombing for which he was sentenced to death was the Muzaffarpur bombing which resulted in the deaths of three persons—Mrs Kennedy (the wife of barrister Pringle Kennedy), her daughter and a servant. After the incident, the revolutionary duo fled. Prafulla committed suicide when cornered by police at the Samastipur Railway station. Khudiram was later arrested. Pretence of a trial was carried out for two months. The leading Calcutta advocate, Narendra Kumar Basu, mounted a stout defence of Khudiram's actions for the freedom of his motherland without charging any fees. In the end, the magistrate read his judgment sentencing Khudiram to death. Even when the judgment was being read, Khudiram did not betray a faint trace of fear. The judge was surprised that a boy of nineteen years accepted death so calmly. 'Do you know what this judgment means?' he asked. Khudiram replied with a smile, 'I know its meaning better than you.' The judge asked, 'Have you anything to say?' 'Yes, I have to explain a few things about making bombs.'

The judge became nervous that Khudiram might make a statement explaining how to make bombs and thus teach everyone in the court to do so. Hence, he did not allow the boy to make a statement. Kalidas Bose yearned to save Khudiram and appealed to the Calcutta High Court but it only confirmed the sentence. Thus, Khudiram's fate was sealed. The sentence was carried out and he was hanged on 11 August 1908 with a copy of the *Bhagavad Gita* in his hand and the slogan *Vande Mataram* on his lips. However, what surprised everyone was that as he was being hanged he was still calm and even smiling. The Bengali poet Kaji Nazrul Islam wrote a poem in honour of the martyr.

Right from the day when Khudiram became a martyr, Kingsford had no peace of mind. Each moment seemed to bring him death. At last, he was so terrified that he resigned his post and settled at Mussoorie. Thus, while Kingsford had to quit his post, the British had to quit India itself. Khudiram not only sacrificed himself but also inspired others by his passion for the cause of freedom for his motherland. A number of young Indians followed his footsteps on the sands of time and played a significant role in ending the British regime in India. He was probably the youngest of the revolutionaries to lay down his life and his courage, dignity and resolve will always be remembered in times to come.

Ram Prasad Bismil

*I*ndian poets also played an important role in the freedom struggle. They gave concepts and visions of freedom. The revolutionary freedom fighters gave shape and content to these concepts and visions. In north India, the freedom poetry of Ajit Singh, Nandlal Noorpuri and Ram Prasad Bismil formed the immortal words of revolt and freedom that inspired mass movements and revolutionary activities of the great Punjabi freedom fighters. Ajit Singh's *Pagri Sambhal O Jatta, Pagri Sambhal Oye, Loot Leya Maal Tera, Haal Behal Oye*, stirred the peasants by depicting their plight and exploitation. It addressed the farmer to awaken, realise how he was being looted and improve his condition. In Punjab, it was considered the first song of freedom and revolt. Similarly, *Aithon Ud Ja Bholya Panchhia* movement of Noorpuri, which was also included into a popular Punjabi film of the times used the cinematic medium to depict the plight of men and women of Punjab under the British rule. And then there was yet another song, *Mera Rang De Basanti Chola*, (O Mother! Dye my robe the colour of spring) which gave birth to one of the greatest and glorious freedom myths. It became Bhagat Singh's song of the gallows. He was said to have marched to the hangman's chamber with this song on his lips. For him death in the cause of freedom was like a celebration. In the Bollywood movie, *The Legend of Bhagat Singh*, Bismil, played by Ganesh Yadav, is depicted as a visionary who ignites in Bhagat Singh the passion for freedom. Two immortal songs from Bengal (Bankim Chandsra's *Vande Mataram* and Rabindranath Tagore's *Jana Gana Mana Adhinayak Jaye Hey*) that stirred the nation also awakened Indians for freedom struggle.

Out of all these poets, Ram Prasad Bismil combined in himself the talents of patriotic poetry and passion to free his country from the slavery of the colonial rule. He was a brave freedom fighter adopting revolutionary means and gave up his life smilingly for the sake of his motherland. 'Bismil' was his pen name. As Bismil, he is well known as a great revolutionary poet in Hindi. Every line of his poems throbs with patriotic fervour. He learnt Hindi from his father and was sent to learn Urdu from a *Moulvi* (muslim tutor). He wanted to join an English medium school and was admitted in one of such schools despite his father's disapproval. Later, he joined Arya Samaj. He acquired the skill of writing fine poetry. All his poems have the intense patriotic feelings. He always wanted to see India as a free nation and dedicated himself to the cause of the country. He became an activist of Arya Samaj, a revolutionary and an associate of Chandrasekhar Azad, Bhagawati Charan and Ashfaqulla Khan. He joined the youth in response to the call of Lala Lajpat Rai to join the freedom struggle against the British.

Ram Prasad was born in the year 1897 at Shahjahanpur, Uttar Pradesh in north India. Bismil is his pseudonym. His ancestors hailed from the state of Gwalior. He was the son of Muralidhar who worked in the municipality of Shahjahanpur. He was the second of two siblings.

The practice of Brahmacharya inspired Ram Prasad and he became its ardent follower. He volunteered himself to the service of Shahjahanpur Seva Samiti. With a view to draw people's attention he published a pamphlet, 'A Message to My Countrymen'. He translated a number of Bengali books. His published works include *The Bolshevik Programme, A Sally of the Mind, Swadeshi Rang*, and *Catherine*. In addition to these books, he also translated *Yogic Sadhana of Rishi Aurobindo*.

Ram Prasad was a member of the Arya Samaj. He felt convinced that 'bombs cannot secure our purpose'. He inspired the youth through his poetry to join him in the struggle through revolutionary means. He was prosecuted by the British Government. He joined the select band of martyrs who dreamt of a free India and made the supreme sacrifice so that the dream might come true. Along with stalwarts like Ashfaqulla Khan, Chandrasekhar Azad, Bhagawati Charan, Rajguru and others he organised several upheavals against the British. They printed literature, provided shelter to revolutionaries, made hand bombs and participated in Kakori train robbery and the bombing of the Punjab Assembly.

In one of his poems, written just before going to the gallows, he prays: 'Oh Lord! Thy will be done. You are unique. Neither my tears nor I will endure. Grant me this boon that on my last breath and the last drop of my blood, I may think of you and be immersed in your work.' His following poem is even now remembered for igniting the minds of Indians to lay down their lives braving through all kinds of difficulties.

Sar faroshi ki tamanna ab hamaare dil mein hai,
Dekhna hai zor kitna baazoo-e-qaatil main hai!

Rahraw-e-rah-e-mohabbat rah na jana rah mein,
Lazzat-e-sahra nawardi doori-e-manzil mein hai.
Yoon khara maqtal mein qaatil kah raha hai baar baar,
Kya tamanna-e-shahaadat bhi kisi ke dil mein hai
Waqt aane par bata denge 'tujhe ai aasmaan,
Hum abhi se kya bataaen kya hamaare dil mein hai.
Ai shaheed-e-mulk-o-millat tere jazbon par nissar,
Teri qurbaani ka charcha ghair ki mehfil mein hai.
Kheinch kar laai hai sabko qatal hone ki umeed,
Aashiqon ka aaj jamghat koocha-e-qaatil mein hai.
Ek se karta nahin koi doosra koi bhi baat,
Dekhta hoon main jise who chup tiri mehfil mein hai.

Which means: 'We are now raring to die for our country's sake. Let's see how much of strength the assassin can display! O traveller on the path of love, do not drop midway. It is the distance of the goal that glorifies the chase. Standing by the gallows the hangman makes a call: "come, if there be any, by the martyr's zeal enthralled. We will tell you all, O sky, wait till the time arrives, how can we at this stage, unveil our secret plans? O martyrs in the nation's cause, kudos to your sacrifice. Even in the enemy camp they talk of you with praise." Fired by patriotic fervour, many maddened youths have gathered at the crossing, itching for the cross. Why are they mute and silent? No whisper, no talk. Everyone that I see has got his lips locked.'

It was the evening of 9 August 1925; the number eight down train was passing near Kakori. Ram Prasad and his nine revolutionary followers pulled the chain and stopped it, looting the money belonging to the British Government. Except one passenger, who was killed by an accidental shot, there was no bloodshed. The dacoity was well-planned.

It jolted the British Government and opened their eyes to the network, organisation and planning of the revolutionaries. After a month of detailed preliminary inquiries and elaborate preparations, the Government cast its net wide for the revolutionaries. Arrest warrants were issued against the ten participants and some leaders of the Hindustan Republican Association. Except Chandrashekhar Azad, all other members of the group were arrested. Ram Prasad Bismil along with others were given capital punishment. Ram Prasad was executed on 19 December 1927. As Bhagat Singh noted, while in prison, Ram Prasad was a man with a soul. Pandit Ram Prasad Bismil will be remembered forever for his bravery, passion for freedom and contribution in the Independence struggle of India.

Rash Behari Bose

On 12 December 1912, five persons joined a huge procession organised to welcome Lord Hardinge. As the entourage reached Khulya Katra, near Chandni Chowk in Delhi, a powerful bomb exploded. Twenty people died on the spot but the main target, Lord Hardinge, managed to escape. In the manhunt that followed, Amir Chand, Avadh Behari, Bal Mukund, and Basanta Biswas were rounded up, and later hanged. But the most daring and the most charismatic of them all, Rash Behari Bose, managed to escape the police dragnet because of his flawless disguise and machinations. Rash Behari Bose, a selfless patriot and the founder of Indian National Army, was a revolutionary leader. Determined to bring the British Raj in India to an end, he dedicated his life to this cause. He played a vital role in India's struggle for Independence. His organisational skills and wonderful spirit of sacrifice greatly contributed towards India's independence.

Rash Behari was born on 25 May 1886 in Subaldana village in Burdwan district in Bengal in undivided India. He was the eldest of a family of four children of Binod Behari Bose, a clerk in the Government Press at Patna. Right from his student days, Rash Behari was an active member of the *Yugantar* group of revolutionaries. He took more interest in organising revolutionary activities than in his studies. Even as a student, he learnt the tricks of making crude bombs and refused to go to college.

The Bengal wing of the revolutionary party sent Rash Behari to Dehradun for converting members of the Indian army to the revolutionary cult. He joined the Forest Research Institute there as a junior officer and tried to raise recruits from among the Bengali residents in Dehradun. He maintained close contacts with the revolutionary leaders in Bengal and Punjab. Rash Behari's job in the Forest Department came in handy for him to execute his plans of manufacturing bombs and directing the revolutionary movement from places which the Government did not suspect and could not easily locate. Soon he emerged as the virtual leader of the revolutionary movement in north India and was an effective link between the revolutionaries of Punjab and Uttar Pradesh on one hand and of Bengal on the other. He toured the whole of north India and visited north India and Bengal to mobilise the revolutionary movement. With a view to organise the movement, he convened a meeting of the workers of various revolutionary groups and formed a central working committee.

When the British Government found surge in the revolutionary activities in Bengal, they decided to change the capital from Calcutta (now Kolkata) to Delhi. Delhi was also made the seat of the Viceroy instead of Calcutta. On 23 December 1912, Lord Hardinge entered Delhi with great pomp and show. Rash Behari and his colleagues planned to throw a bomb on the viceregal procession. The bomb routed the elephant, killed one of the ADCs and caused bloodshed. Everybody believed that the Viceroy had been killed but he had a lucky escape.

The people of Central Intelligence as well as the Scotland Yard started investigation but in spite of their best efforts they could not trace the person who had masterminded the whole incident. The only clue they could gather was that a young Muslim damsel, wrapped in a veil, had thrown something from the top of the Punjab National Bank building in Chandni Chowk. After accomplishing his task, Rash Behari, with a view to hoodwink the police, addressed a public meeting at Dehradun and criticised the bomber. He also offered his services to the CID to help them find out the culprit. They too readily welcomed the young Bengali's offer to help since it had all along been believed that it was the work of a Bengali revolutionary. But when Rash Behari felt that he might be apprehended, he went underground. After intensive investigations, thirteen persons were sentenced to various terms of imprisonment. Rash Behari, the chief accused, could not be apprehended.

During the World War, the Gadar Party, under the leadership of Lala Har Dayal, started recruiting Indians in America to be sent to India for uprising against the British. The German submarines were to supply arms and ammunition to the revolutionary forces. The Gadar Party approached Rash Behari through Bhai Parmanand and entrusted him the task of guiding the Gadar revolutionaries who reached India. Rash Behari had by then made Benaras his headquarters. He undertook the task of organising the mass uprising in the north and established contact with Indian soldiers in the cantonments of north India. He persuaded them to take part in the revolt. Many other leaders also joined Rash Behari. 21 February 1916 was fixed as the day for uprising. But an agent of the British, Kripal Singh, had sneaked into the organisation. Rash Behari, with his sharp acumen, recognised Kripal Singh and wanted the revolutionaries to do away with him. But his colleagues, out of human consideration, ignored Rash Behari's warning. Kirpal Singh escaped. The plan came to the notice of the British and the movement was suppressed.

Rash Behari alerted the revolutionaries, who were waiting for 21 February, in the East. He stayed for a month in the crowds of the police and secret spies, eluding them all. Barrister J.M.J Chatterji arranged some finance for him and Rash Behari set his voyage to Japan under a British passport and under the assumed name of Raja P.N. Tagore after presenting to the Commissioner of Police, Calcutta, as one of Gurudev Tagore's secretaries, proceeding to Japan to make arrangements for his visit to Tokyo.

Rash Behari reached Tokyo in June 1915. He convened a meeting of the sponsors of the Indian Freedom Movement on 25 November. The meeting was attended by some revolutionaries, Japanese sympathisers and Lala Lajpat Rai. The meeting aroused the sympathy of the Japanese people for the efforts of the revolutionaries. But in pursuance of the conditions of the Anglo-Japanese alliance, the Japanese Government was forced to direct Rash Behari and his associate, Hermbalal Gupta, to leave Japan before 2 December. But the Japanese people and the press came out openly in support of Rash Behari. A political leader, Mitsui Toyama, assured help and protection to Rash Behari. Consequently, he was provided with a secret hiding place in the cellar of an influential hotel. Three months later, a British man-of-war attacked a Japanese ship, and this provoked the Japanese Government to hit at the British pride and prestige by reversing its policy in regard to Rash Behari. During his stay in Naka Muraya, Mr and Mrs Zoma, who bestowed on him loving care, developed a filial affection for Rash Behari. They offered their eldest daughter, Tosiko, in marriage to Rash Behari. Even after marriage, Rash Behari never forgot his Motherland and he continued his militant activities. Toshiko passed away in 1920 after she suffered from the exhaustion of an unstable life with the anti-government activist.

On 15 February 1942, during the Second World War, Singapore fell into the hands of Japan. Japanese arrested 15,000 British, 13,000 Australian and 32,000 Indian soldiers. All of them were taken as prisoners of war. Japan also took over Malaya and established her authority over the country of five million people, among whom three hundred thousand were Indians. Subhash Chandra Bose, who was then in Germany and was finding it difficult to move forces from the European theatre to the Indian borders, looked to Japan for help in opening an Eastern Front. At this juncture, Rash Behari thought of a plan. He inspired the captured Indians to form a Liberation Army and invade India from outside. On 17 February 1942, just after the conquest of Singapore, Major Fujiwara, Commander of the victorious Japanese army, summoned the prominent Indian citizens in Singapore, and told them that if they were prepared to renounce their British citizenship and organise themselves for the fight for the freedom of India, Japan would provide assistance. Rash Behari convened a conference of the representatives of Indians in Japan, China, Malaya and Thailand in Tokyo on 28 March and formed the Indian Independence League. A plan to build up Azad Hind Fauj on the pattern of the Free India Army of Berlin was also announced.

There was another conference of Indians in Bangkok from 14 June to 23 June where representatives of millions of Indians scattered all over Java, Sumatra, Indo-China, Borneo, Manchuko, Hong Kong, Burma, Malaya and Japan congregated. The conference presented a memorandum to Japan requesting that its demand for equal rights and status for the Azad Hind Fauj of Free India be conceded. The meeting also constituted the War Council of the League with Rash Behari as its first President. The conference also decided to invite Subhash Chandra Bose to lead the Indian Independence League and the Azad Hind Fauj in the East, and an invitation was sent accordingly. After this, the membership of the League swelled to 120,000; 50,000 Indian soldiers were enlisted in the Indian National Army. An independent broadcasting centre was also set up at Bangkok.

Subhash Chandra Bose reached Tokyo in a submarine on 20 June. On 2 July, he reached Singapore where the Indians, Chinese and the Japanese accorded him an unprecedented welcome. He gave the call to Indians gathered there: *'Chalo Dilli'* (march to Delhi). On 5 July 1943, Subhash Chandra Bose was made the President of Indian Independence League and Rash Behari became his adviser. Soon, Rani Laxmi Regiment was formed with Laxmi Sehgal as its Captain.

Rash Behari Bose died of heart attack on 21 January 1945 and thus ended the saga of a great patriot of India. He was cremated by Buddhist rites and his ashes were buried in Yama Cemetry. His son, Masahide Bose, was killed in action while fighting for the Japanese Army in Okinawa. In 1958, when the ashes of Rash Behari were brought to India by his daughter, Tetsu Higuchi, Dr Rajendra

Prasad, the then President of India, paid a glowing tribute and described him as one of those well-known patriots whose love for the Motherland and burning desire to see her free could never be curbed. Before his death, the Japanese Government honoured Rash Behari with the 'Second Order of the Merit of the Rising Sun'.

Shivaram Rajguru

$\mathcal{H}$ ari Shivaram Rajguru was a great Indian revolutionary who sacrificed his life for the emancipation of India from the British colonial rule. He was a close associate of the revolutionary leader, Bhagat Singh. Rajguru, as he came to be known famously, was born on 23 March 1931 at Varanasi in Uttar Pradesh in north India. He was the son of Hari Rajguru of Poona. He belonged to the Deshastha Brahmin community in Maharashtra. Since his childhood days, he had witnessed the brutal atrocities that the imperial British Raj inflicted on India and her people. This instilled in him a strong urge to join hands with the revolutionaries in a bid for India's freedom struggle.

The protest against the Simon Commission in October 1928 saw the British police lathi-charge the protestors, severely injuring veteran leader Lala Lajpat Rai. Owing to the excessive beating, Lala Lajpat Rai succumbed to his injuries. This enraged Rajguru and he joined hands with Bhagat Singh and Sukhdev to take revenge against the British police.

During those days, the Hindustan Socialist Republican Army (HSRA) was an active force working against the British. While the Army's main objective was to strike fear in the British regime, they also wanted to bring in awareness among the Indians. Rajguru joined this Army. On 17 December 1928, he was accomplice in the assassination of J.P. Saunders, Deputy Superintendent of police, spearheaded by Bhagat Singh. On 8 April 1929, he participated in the planting of bomb in the Central Assembly Hall in New Delhi along with Bhagat Singh and Sukhdev. However, on 30 September 1929, during his travel to Poona, in a motor garage, Rakguru was finally arrested. He was tried as one of the principal accused in the Lahore Conspiracy Case of 1930.

On 23 March 1931, the three brave revolutionaries were hanged in the Lahore Central Jail. Their bodies were cremated on the banks of the River Sutlej. Rajguru was only twenty-year-old when he became a martyr for his country. However, he remains to be one of the shining stars in the list of great Indian revolutionaries.

Sukhdev Thapar

Sukhdev, an accomplice of Bhagat Singh and Shivaram Rajguru and an Indian revolutionary, played a great role for the freedom of his country. He embodied tremendous courage, patriotism and self-sacrifice and has been rightly commemorated with the recent naming of a school after him in his native city Ludhiana, Punjab in north India.

Sukhdev was born on 15 May 1907 in Naughara Mohalla of Ludhiana city, Punjab in north India. He was the son of Ram Lal. Not much is known about his education and upbringing except that since his childhood days, he had witnessed the brutal atrocities that the imperial British Raj had inflicted on India. This made him anguish and join the revolutionaries and take a vow to join the revolutionaries and make it free from the shackles of British dominion

Sukhdev became a member of the Hindustan Socialist Republican Association (HSRA) and organised revolutionary cells in Punjab and other areas of north India. He was a devoted leader. He started study circles at the National College in Lahore to delve deep into India's past and explore the finer aspects of world revolutionary literature and the Russian Revolution so as to educate the youth. He inspired young people about India's glorious past. He joined Bhagat Singh, Comrade Ram Chandra and Bhagwati Charan Vohra in the setting up of the Naujawan Bharat Sabha at Lahore, an organisation involved in various activities. With this his purpose was to activate youth for freedom struggle and inculcate in them a rational scientific attitude, fight communalism and end the practice of untouchability.

He himself participated in several revolutionary activities like the 'Prison hunger strike' in 1929 to protest against the inhuman treatment of inmataes. However, he will always be remembered for his daring yet courageous attacks in the Lahore Conspiracy Case on 18 December 1928. This episode scared the British Government. In 1928, he accompanied Bhagat Singh and Shivaram Rajguru in the assassination of J.P. Saunders, Deputy Superintendent of Police, in avenging the death of Lala Lajpat Rai. On 8 April 1929, he planned and executed bombings of the Central Assembly Hall with the help of other revolutionaries. He was arrested and convicted of crime. As a result, on 23 March 1931, he, along with three brave revolutionaries, Bhagat Singh, Sukhdev Thapar and Shivaram Rajguru, was hanged at 7.30 pm against all norms of hanging. The dead bodies were surreptitiously taken away by breaking the back walls of the jail. Their bodies were secretly cremated on the banks of the River Sutlej near Firozepur about fifty miles away from Lahore. The bodies were cut into pieces to make the cremation quick.

Sukhdev thus martyred himself at the tender age of twenty-four. He will always be remembered for his courage, patriotism and sacrifice of his life for India's independence.

Mangal Pandey

Ketan Mehta's film, *Mangal Pandey: The Rising* (2005), starring Aamir Khan along with Rani Mukherji, Toby Stephens and Amish Patel again brought to focus the indomitable spirit and sacrifice of Mangal Pandey, the hero of the First War of Indian Independence. It continues to remind the succeeding generations the role of Mangal Pandey in India's freedom movement. Although the film dramatises the life and actions of Mangal Pandey in an extensive manner, it vividly recaptures the major incident which culminated in the Rebellion—the shooting of a British officer by Mangal Pandey, then a soldier in the British Army. Subsequently, he was captured, tried and hanged to death. Mangal Pandey was a fearless and revolutionary soldier who championed the cause of India's resurgence. His martyrdom provided a much needed fillip to the 1857 Rebellion and caused its subsequent outbreak in other parts of the country as well.

Mangal Pandey was born on 19 July 1927 in the village of Nagwa in district Ballia of Uttar Pradesh in north India. Families in Nagwa village claim Mangal to be their first ancestor and trace their family lineage to him. However, there is some dispute over Mangal's exact place of birth. Some people say that Mangal was born in a Bhumihar

Brahmin family of Divakar Pandey of Surhupur village of Faizabad district's Akbar Tehsil. Not much is known about Mangal's upbringing and education. He joined the British East India forces in 1849 at the age of twenty-two. He was a soldier in the 5th Company of the 34th BNI regiment.

A new type of bullet cartridge used in the Enfield P-53 rifle was to be introduced in the Bengal Army. There was a rumour that the cartridge was greased with animal fat, primarily pig fat and cow fat. The cartridges had to be bitten at one end prior to use. Since both Muslims and Hindus do not consume such animals, Hindu and Muslim soldiers in the Army felt that the Britishers had intentionally resorted to this kind of cartridge to hurt their religious susceptibilities. Again, it was also felt that Britishers were poised to promote Christianity in India.

This became evident when the soldiers found that Commandant Wheeler of the 34th BNI happened to be a devout Christian and with a view to spread Christianity among the soldiers he arranged translation of the Bible in Urdu and Nagri and got the copies distributed among the sepoys (soldiers). The soldiers felt convinced about the missionary idea of the Britishers.

Yet, what irritated the soldiers further was the annexation of Oudh by the Nawab on 7 February 1856. A significant portion of the Bengal Army hailed from the princely state. Before the annexation, these sepoys had the right to petition the British Resident at Lucknow for justice—a privilege in the context of native courts. As a result of the annexation, they lost that right since that state no longer existed. Moreover, this action was seen by the residents of the state as an affront to their honour, the annexation being done in violation of an existing treaty.

In this way, the simmering discontent among the sepoys in particular and people in general became visible when non-commissioned officers of the regiment refused to accept the cartridges on 26 February 1857 on looking at a different paper used in the cartridges. The irritation among the soldiers was brought to the notice of the commanding officer, Colonel Mitchell, who tried to convince the sepoys that the cartridges were no different from those they had been accustomed to and they need not bite it. He even threatened to court martial the sepoys refusing to accept the cartridge. However, there was a rebellion in the regiment next morning. The soldiers were asked to return to barracks. A court of enquiry was ordered. As a result, the regiment was disbanded.

On 29 March 1857, at Barrackpore, near Calcutta (now, Kolkata), Lieutenant Baugh, Adjutant of the 34th Native Infantry was informed that several persons of his regiment were in an excited mood. It was brought to his notice that one Mangal Pandey had incited his colleagues to rebel. He himself threatened to shoot the first European he encountered. Immediately on hearing this, Baugh mounted his horse and galloped to the lines. When he came towards Mangal, the latter started firing. Though he missed Baugh but the bullet struck his horse. Baugh also fired, but missed Mangal. Mangal attacked Baugh with a sword. Another sepoy intervened and tried to restrain Mangal.

An English Sergeant-Major reached the spot. In the altercation that ensued between some soldiers and English commanders, Mangal was arrested. Before this he fought valiantly and was wounded. After he recovered, he was brought to trial less than a week later. When asked whether he had been under the influence of any substances, he admitted to having used *bhang* (an Indian drug) and opium and when intoxicated he did not know what he was doing. He stated steadfastly that he had mutinied on his own accord and that none had instigated him. He was sentenced to death by hanging. His execution was scheduled for April 18, but was carried out ten days prior to that date on April 21.

The 34th N.I. Regiment was disbanded 'with disgrace' on May 6 as a collective punishment after a detailed investigation by the Government for failing to perform their duty in restraining a mutinous soldier and protecting their officer. This came after a period of six weeks in the course of which petitions for leniency were examined in Calcutta. Shaikh Paltu, the person who had helped the commanders in arresting Mangal Pandey, was promoted to the post of Havaldar (native sergeant) by General Hearsay for his gallant conduct.

Though Mangal Pandey is no more, yet he will always be remembered as a brave soldier. During a fierce battle in one of the Afghan wars that the Britishers fought in the mid-century, the heroic sepoy saved the life of his British commanding officer, William Gordon. Gordon remained indebted to Mangal and a strong friendship developed between them, transcending considerations of rank and race.

Mangal Pandey was a great revolutionary who ignited the first spark of India's freedom struggle and who laid down his precious life for his country's emancipation. The film, *Mangal Pandey: The Rising*, one of Bollywood's grandest epic movies to date, rightfully commemorates the deeds of the great revolutionary. Similarly, the life of Mangal Pandey was also the subject of a stage play titled *The Roti Rebellion* which was written and directed by Supriya

Karunakaran. The play organised by Sparsh, a theatre group, was presented in June 2005 at the Moving Theatre at Andhra Saraswat Parishad, Hyderabad, Andhra Pradesh. As a fitting tribute to the great revolutionary, the Government of India rightfully commemorated Mangal Pandey by issuing a postage stamp bearing his image on 5 October 1984. The stamp and the accompanying first-day cover were designed by Delhi-based artist C.R. Pakrashi. Mangal Pandey's sacrifice and bravery earned him an immortal place in the hearts of his fellow Indians.

Madan Lal Dhingra

Madan Lal Dhringra was an Indian political activist and a revolutionary who sacrificed his life for the cause of Indian independence. Like Vinayak Damodar Savarkar and Shyamji Krishnavarma, Dhingra too believed in revolutionary methods for attaining freedom.

Madan Lal was born in 1887 in a prosperous Hindu family in the province of Punjab. His father was a wealthy civil surgeon. He studied at Amritsar and Lahore. He worked for sometime in Bombay (now Mumbai) before acting upon the advice of his elder brother and going to England for higher studies. In 1906, he joined the University College of Engineering in London to study Mechanical Engineering. He was supported by his elder brother and some nationalist activists in England.

Madan Lal came in contact with Indian political activists, Vinayak Damodar Savarkar and Shyamji Krishnavarma, who were impressed by Madan Lal's perseverance and intense patriotism. Soon he turned his focus to the freedom struggle. Savarkar believed in revolution by any means, and supposedly gave Madan arms training, apart from membership in a secretive society, the *Abhinav Bharat Sanstha*. He was also a member of India

House, the base for Indian student political activity. Savarkar, Madan Lal and other student activists were enraged by the execution of freedom fighters such as Khudiram Bose, Kannai Dutt, Satinder Pal and Kanshi Ram in India. These events, it is believed, led Savarkar and Madan Lal to plan for revenge against the British.

While in England, Madan Lal took part in Indian revolutionary activities in Britain. He undertook training in the use of fire arms. His family members, who owed allegiance to the British, disowned him because of his revolutionary activities. Consequently, he had to work as a clerk, a *tonga* (horse-driven carriage) puller, and a factory labourer but it did not deter him from his mission. He attempted to organise a union in England, but was sacked by the university.

On 1 July 1909, a large number of Indians and Englishmen assembled to attend the annual day function of the Indian National Association in India House. When Sir Curzon Wyllie, political aide-de-camp to the Secretary of State for India, entered the hall with his wife, Madan Lal fired five shots right at his face, four of which hit the target. Cowasji Lalkaka, a Parsee doctor, who tried to save Sir Curzon, also died of Madan Lal's sixth and seventh bullets. Madan Lal tried to commit suicide by turning his pistol on himself but was apprehended after a brief altercation.

On 23 July 1909, Madan Lal was tried in the Old Bailey Court. He stated that he did not intend to kill Cowasji Lalkaka. Nevertheless, he was sentenced to death. After the judge announced his verdict, Madan Lal Dhingra is said to have stated: 'I am proud to have the honour of laying down my life for my country. But remember, we shall have our time in the days to come.' He was hanged on 17 August 1909. His body was denied Hindu rites and he was buried by the British authorities. His family having disowned him, the authorities refused to turn over the body to Savarkar. Madan Lal's body was, however, accidently found while the authorities were searching for the remains of Shaheed Udham Singh. His remains were subsequently repatriated to India on 13 December 1976. The August issue of *The Indian Sociologist* carried a story sympathetic to Madan Lal Dhingra. Mahatma Gandhi, however, condemned Madan Lal Dhingra's actions. His actions evoked some sympathy from the Irish who were fighting their own struggle at that time. Some modern historians claim that the trial was grossly unfair and biased. Madan Lal was not given even a defence counsel and the entire process was completed in a single day. Madan Lal Dhingra will always be remembered as a great martyr along with Bhagat Singh and Chandrasekhar Azad. He was one of the first revolutionaries to lay down his life and pave the way for the freedom of his motherland.

Senapati Bapat

Senapati Bapat, whose original name was Pandurang Mahadev Bapat, was a great revolutionary. He participated in the armed and unarmed struggles for India's emancipation from the British colonial regime. He was known for his progressive ideas. He did pioneering work in the eradication of untouchability. Widely known as *Senapati* (commander of armed forces) because of his leadership of the Mulshi Satyagraha campaign in the early twenties he was incarcerated for almost twenty years from time to time. His sacrifice and self-service provides an insight into the turbulent times he lived.

Pandurang Bapat was born on 12 November 1880 in a Chitpawan or Konkanastha Brahmin family at Parner in the Ahmednagar district of the Bombay Presidency. Pandurang's father, Mahadeorao, who was deeply religious and an ardent devotee of Lord Ganesha, continued the family tradition of looking after the temple. Pandurang was fourth of the six children of his parents. The Bapat family was a lower middle class family and his members inevitably had to face poverty and hardship.

As a child, Pandurang preferred games to academic. He impressed his teachers in the primary school at Parner by his intelligence and prodigious memory. He studied in New English School. In 1898, he married a nine-year old girl, Yamuna Moreshwar Bhane who was named Rukhmini after marriage. Pandurang passed his high school examination after marriage. He joined Deccan College in 1890 and passed his Bachelors degree in 1893. It was here that he first came in contact with revolutionaries. In 1904, he went to Edinburgh in Scotland to study mechanical engineering. There he joined Harriot-Watt College at Edinburgh.

In Edinburgh, he presented a paper on 'British Rule in India' at one of the meetings organised by the local branch of the Independent Labour Party. He declared that the yearning for self-government had become 'a part and parcel of the educated Indian mind'. Due to his provocative address, the University of Bombay, on whose scholarship he had come to Edinburgh, expelled him. Savarkar, who arrived in London on scholarship, criticised the withdrawal of scholarship by the University. Revolution became Pandurang's priority.

His articles were published in *Vande Mataram*. He presented a paper in Edinburgh on 'India in the Year 2007', where he explained his philosophy of killing and justified the use of violence for ensuring justice. He met Anna in Berlin and collected English translation of the Russian manual on making bombs. This facilitated his revolutionary colleagues in manufacturing picric acid and carrying out experiments for making bombs. The Bomb Manual was later used extensively in India by the revolutionaries. Police became suspicious and a cash-prize was offered to any one who gave information about his whereabouts. In 1909, he accepted the job of a compositor in a printing press in Badhwani. He was interrogated by the police in 1912 but no prima facie case could be established against him.

Pandurang studied the Upanishads and the works of Shankaracharya. He read the *Bhagavad Gita* many times and made careful study of the Bible and the Quran. He read the works of Swami Vivekananda, Swami Ramatirtha and Sri Aurobindo. He also studied the works of the medieval Marathi Saint poets including Ramdas and Tukaram. All this convinced him about the existence of God and that human being is required to play a role assigned by Him. He preached the gospel of broom, spent several hours each day cleaning latrines and streets even in areas occupied by the so-called untouchables. He felt that in this way he was serving God. In August 1893, he began teaching children of the 'untouchables', In August 1915, he joined the *Mahratta* as an assistant editor.

In April 1921, Pandurang joined the S*atyagraha* movement to stop the Tata Company from laying a railway line but when the Tatas didn't agree, he removed the line. He and his friends were found guilty by the court and Pandurang was imprisoned for six months. He clarified that the achievement of *swarajya* or *swatantra* was impossible if Indians resorted to only peaceful and non-violence methods. In one of his poems, he declared that it was their duty to kill wicked people. He was imprisoned in October 1923 for one year, and again for seven years. He cheerfully spent this period in jail cleaning latrines and composing verses.

On 26 May 1931, in his speech, he pleaded that India must establish a republic as widely democratic in form as possible. He proposed that India should have a Presidential form of Government and the first President of the Republic should be a Muslim. He suggested that every President should hold office for four years and at the end of forty years the Constitution should be revised. He was often critical of the Congress and its mild programmes. Yet, the Gandhians in Maharashtra Pradesh Congress Committee decided to elect him as the President of the MPCC. He warned the people that they could not force the British to quit India by boycotting foreign goods or by spinning or by introducing prohibition.

He criticised the national leaders who were weakening the freedom movement by their squabble and emphasised the need to promote Hindu-Muslim unity, which was a key to the solution to India's political problems. Unlike other politicians, he did not try to build a group of his own supporters. He spent good deal of his time in cleaning streets and latrines. In October 1937, he led a campaign to clean the city of Poona.

In October/November 1937, he threatened to commit suicide by drowning in the river. He continued to recommend the idea of self-inflicted death for more than a decade. In March 1938, he decided to join the Indian National Congress. He did not approve of Savarkar's attitude towards the Muslims. His views on social, political and economic issues were broadly leftist and he personally preferred to be called a moderate socialist. He advised the younger generation to 'study Moscow". He maintained that abolition of British rule in India was necessary for the elimination of poverty in India. He favoured the establishment of a semi-socialist society after the achievement of freedom.

In 1938, Pandurang participated in the Satyagraha campaign in the princely state of Hyderabad. In December 1938, he was sentenced to two years' rigorous imprisonment. In August 1939, he took over as the President of the

Maharashtra Branch of the Forward Bloc and advocated a policy of non-cooperation with the British. In February 1940, he defied the ban on public meetings in the princely state of Kolhapur. He was arrested twice.

Imprisonment for several years as well as old age had effects on his body but he remained cheerful. Though reading proved quite strenuous, he read several books. He read *Brihadaranyaka* (Hindi), Vivekananda's works, *Groundwork of Educational Psychology*, Stont's *Manual of Psychology*, *Gitarahasaya*, and many other books. He translated Aurobindo's *Life Divine* and other works into Marathi.

When India attained Independence, Senapati Pandurang Bapat was given the honour to hoist flag at the Congress House on the first Independence Day. Following Mahatma Gandhi's assassination on 30 January 1948 the houses of Hindu Mahasabha and RSS were set on fire. Senapati Pandurang Bapat tried to restore sanity. He showed exemplary courage by boldly facing a howling mob in Ahmednagar. He didn't tolerate any injustice. In September 1950, he undertook a fast for eight days as a protest against the dismissal of two school teachers. On 13 May 1952, at the age of seventy-two he participated in the Satyagraha campaign against the rising prices organised by the Praja Socialist Party. In 1953, when Maharashtra suffered from severe famine he was elected President of the Bombay Committee for organising famine relief.

In July 1949, he formed Samyukta Maharashtra Mahamandal for the demand of separate state of Maharashtra. At one stage, he favoured militant line of action, though, later on, he dropped the idea. He had kept in touch with former revolutionaries who had earlier made gallant efforts to wage an armed struggle. In May 1955, he led a batch of 38 Satyagrahis to Goa. The police resorted to firing and Senapati Pandurang Bapat narrowly escaped. On 18 November 1955, he led a batch of more than five hundred Satyagrahis in Bombay, defied the ban on public meetings and was arrested. He was released the next day. His Satyagraha and arrest marked the beginning of a particularly stormy phase in the Samyukta Maharashtra movement in which there was an unprecedented outburst of violence and police repression.

With advancing age, Senapati Pandurang Bapat became physically weaker but his fighting spirit was still intact. On 20 May 1966, he undertook fast along with others. Again, when the Mahajan Commission rejected the demand for the inclusion of the city of Belgaun in Maharashtra he announced his plan to go on fast unto death from 21 October 1967 but when persuaded by others he postponed it by one month. On 25 November, he fell in the bathroom and never recovered. He breathed his last on 28 November 1967 .

Thus ended Senapati Pandurang Bapat's eventful career at the age of eighty-seven. He was known for his progressive ideas and ideals in social and economic matters. His patriotic fervour kindled during his formative years at the Deccan College continued to illuminate the path for others till the end of his life. Together with this, his enthusiasm to champion the cause of downtrodden and oppressed and his programme of cleaning the localities have immortalised him as a revolutionary and a freedom fighter with distinct attributes.

M. N. Roy

$\mathcal{M}$.N. Roy was the illustrious founder of the political movement known as Radical Humanism. As a philosophy of life, Radical Humanism covers the entire gamut of human existence from abstract thought to social and political reconstruction. It is the tradition of the revolt of man against the tyranny of God and his agents on this earth. Roy was a great revolutionary and a political activist, who had the unique opportunity of working with revolutionary figures like Lenin, Trotsky and Stalin. He not only participated in the armed struggle in India against the British Empire during the first two decades of twentieth century but also in the revolutionary activities in Mexico and China. It is rare that a political activist happens to be a scholar and a thinker, but Roy was both. With his distinct approach, he differed with Mahatma Gandhi and Jawaharlal Nehru. He had better contacts both within and outside the country than any other leader in India. Even Nehru lacked the experience and vision that Roy possessed of the revolutionary movements in other lands.

The original name of M.N. Roy was Narendranath Bhattacharya. He was known by this name during the first phase of his life, the phase of militant nationalism.

Narendranath or Naren, as he was known in those days, was born in 1887 in Arbelia, a village not far from Calcutta (now Kolkata) in the district of 24 Parganas. His father, Dinabandhu Bhattacharya, was the head-priest of the temple of Goddess Ksheputeshwari in the village Ksheput in Midnapur district of south-west Bengal. The head-priestship was hereditary in the family. Dinabandhu left the village and took a job as a Sanskrit teacher in the village of Arbelia. Narendranath was the fourth child of his father, and second by his second wife. The child was brought up and educated at Chingripota which also became the scene of his first action as a militant nationalist. Narendranath passed the entrance examination and enlisted himself as a student in National College, Calcutta. During his early years, Narendranath learnt a good deal of Sanskrit from his father, elder brother and others.

While Narendranath was growing up, Bengal was passing through a political ferment. which reached its acme during the days of the agitation against the partition of Bengal in 1905. The idea of motherland evoked by Bankimchandra Chatterji in his famous novel, *Anandmath*, and his slogan of *Vande Mataram*, gripped the mind of Narendranath. Swami Vivekananda, who after his triumphant return from the United States of America, became the powerful spokesman of religious nationalism in the form of resurrected spiritual Hinduism, also influenced his sensitive mind. The young boy was already adventurous, walking long distances and wandering about from orchard to orchard for something distant, something beyond. He used to spend many nights in the cremation ground looking for ghosts. Narendranath was a restless soul. He visited the Ramakrishna Ashram at Belur, met

Sivnarain Swamy and collected information about revolutionaries and their activities.

Even at the young age of fourteen, Narendranath was quite energetic and full of revolutionary enthusiasm. He acquainted himself with the problems in Bengal and offered himself as a whole-timer for the cause of liberty of India from the foreign yoke. He declared on oath that he would be prepared to do the impossible. It was the goal of freedom which drew Naren to the revolutionary movement. In 1905, he started attending anti-partition meetings held frequently in Calcutta along with his friends. On account of their political activism, they were rusticated from college. Later, the order was withdrawn and they were allowed to appear for the entrance examination. Naren and his friends were avid readers of the *Bhagavad Gita, Anandmath, Bhavani Mandir* and other revolutionary literature of the period. But what impressed them most were the writings of Swami Vivekananda.

Naren and his friends joined the Anushilan Samity, an organisation in Calcutta for physical, mental and moral regeneration of Bengali youths. It developed an inner or underground wing which became the centre of revolutionary activities all over Bengal. In course of time, similar organisations were set up in many other towns, some as branches and others as independent centres. During this phase of his life, he came in close contact with Barin Ghosh who had already started the Bengali daily, the *Jugantar*. Naren helped Ghosh in looking after the daily and is said to have written some articles for the newspaper. Later, he wrote a booklet in Bengali entitled *Mayer Dak* (Mother's Call) and when police came to know of this, Naren was arrested. After joining the revolutionary movement he was already initiated into the art of shooting and bomb making. Bullets and bombs were the main instruments of the revolutionaries and were used for terrorising British officers and for punishing defectors from the ranks.

Naren committed the first political dacoity at Chingripota Railway Station on 6 December 1907 to secure funds for the revolutionary activities that had developed under the leadership of Jatin Mukherjee. He was arrested and a copy of Barin Ghosh's *Bartaman Rananiti* (Strategy of Modern Warfare) and the manuscript titled *Mayer Dak* (Mother's Call) were seized from his possession. He was released on bail. In the course of a couple of years, Naren committed more political dacoities. He was arrested on bail and then he absconded. As a fugitive, he spent most of his time in Howrah and Sibpur. Under the leadership of Jatin Mukherjee, he organised a movement. He had political discussions with various groups and planned guerilla type warfare and employed other means to drive the British out of the country. He held socialistic views and never mixed religion with politics. He thought of a 'People's Government' as distinct from the government of the privileged few and he felt convinced that the only way to establish such a government was revolution.

Naren was arrested in Howrah-Sibpur Conspiracy Case and spent about nine months in jail in solitary confinement, the most excruciating experience for him. While in incarceration, Naren along with other revolutionaries drew up a plan of armed insurrection. After his release from the jail, Naren took up employment as agent of the India Equitable Assurance Company. He also worked as a bill collector of a rice mill and a timber workshop. Later, he opened a restaurant which became a centre for procurement of arms and exchange of information. It became popular amongst soldiers and sailors owing to the special dishes that Naren used to cook for them. He undertook the task of uniting all the revolutionaries. He became a *sanyasi* to avoid the suspicion of the police and visited places like Banaras, Allahabad, Agra and Mathura. In about a year, a united organisation was established with branches and contacts in Bengal and outside. It came to be known as the Jugantar Party.

Naren established contacts with Indian revolutionary groups in Europe, the United States of America, Burma (now Myanmar), Indonesia and in places like Bangkok, Singapore, and Hong Kong. In the Western hemisphere, there were strong revolutionary groups in Vancouver in Canada and in San Francisco in the United States. He went to Java, Germany and Indonesia in 1915 as 'C Martin' in search of arms, ostensibly as agent of the Harry & Sons, Calcutta, but somehow or the other his mission failed. He was able to establish contact with Sun Yat-Sen and other leaders of the Chinese Revolution. He went to China. He found himself in British custody for one night in the Chinese city of Tientsin. Towards the end of 1915, there was a revolt in two Chinese provinces of Yunan and Szechuan, bordering on Burma and India. The revolt was against Yuan Shi-kai's plan to restore monarchy. The rebels had plenty of arms. Sun-Yat-Sen liked Naren's suggestion that the Chinese rebels should pass on some of their arms to Indian revolutionaries across the border and get five million dollars from the German Ambassador for the purchase of those arms. If the money was available, Sun Yat-Sen would send his emissary to Yunan and then Naren would proceed to take over the 'precious cargo'. But the plan fell through because at the last moment the Germans were not ready to spend the large amount, which it required.

Naren arrived in the United States of America in June 1916. A newspaper reported that one Charles A. Martin had arrived and though he had declared that he is en route to Paris to study theology, he was believed to be a revolutionary. On learning this, Naren immediately changed his name to M.N. Roy and started his journey to the New World. In Stanford, Roy met many academicians and political workers. He made many friends. There he married Evelyn Trent who helped him in his mission. From now on she became Roy's political collaborator and accompanied him to Mexico and Russia. She co-authored a couple of books with Roy and wrote from time to time for communist journals under the pen-name 'Shantidevi'. This continued till they separated in 1926. Roy also came in contact with many American socialists and Lala Lajpat Rai. In New York, he began a systematic study of socialism. The transition to socialism was a big event in Roy's political career. He continued to work for the revolution. But the revolution that he visualised after his conversion to socialism was basically different from the revolution that he worked for as a militant nationalist. One conceived a new social order, while the other was restricted only to the overthrow of British rule.

- Roy was arrested one day in Columbia University for violating the immigration laws of the U.S.A. He was released on a personal security. He gave a slip to the police in New York and after a two-day train journey landed in Mexico in July 1917 without any money. There he met two German officers whom he had met earlier in Indonesia. He was able to contact the President of the country and was able to secure large funds which he used for developing the Socialist Party of Mexico and later for rendering asistance to Borodin and the Russian Trade Mission in Washington. He contributed articles to a leading daily newspaper, the *El Pueblo*. The articles were written in English and then translated into Spanish, the language of the country. A conference was held in Mexico City in December 1917 and the Socialist Party was launched. Roy was elected its General Secretary. His work was so impressive that nobody believed that Roy was a foreigner. He was required to draft the labour bill and accompany the Labour Minister to various places to pacify workers who were resorting to strikes. He also helped in the editing of the party journal and the building up of the party organisation. The activities of the Socialist Party strengthened and widened the social base of the government. There he developed friendship with Michael Borodin, one of the leaders of the Bolshevik Party of Russia who completed Roy's conversion to communism. Roy learned from him not only the intricacies of dialectical materialism but also the greatness of European civilisation and the appreciation of art and culture. With Roy's help, Borodin succeeded in securing for Bolsheviks a foothold in the New World. Roy presided over a conference which decided to change the name of the party to the Communist Party, the first in the world outside Russia. Thus, Borodin prepared the ground for Roy's visit to Moscow.

Roy left Mexico in November 1919 after spending more than two years. A diplomatic passport was arranged for him. Mexico's representatives in European countries were advised to render him any assistance that he might need. He reached Moscow in April 1920 anxious to work for revolution in India by getting guidance and direction of the centre of world revolution located in Moscow. He was introduced to the leaders of the Comintern, including Lenin, Zinoviev, Trotsky, and Stalin. Lenin complimented Roy on his work in Mexico and stated that it could show the way to communist work in colonies and semi-colonies. Roy attended the second Congress of the Comintern as the representative of the Communist Party of Mexico, but for practical purposes, he was treated as the representative of India. He was elected to various bodies. After the congress adopted the two theses, Roy, Lenin and other leaders had almost identical views. The two theses were quoted frequently in the various phases of the Chinese Revolution. Stalin referred to them twice in May 1927 and contended that Roy's supplementary thesis was more relevant to the situation than Lenin's. The second Congress established Roy's position in the Comintern. Roy was now assigned the task of carrying the revolution to the East and more particularly to India.

The East comprised not only India but the Asian region of Russia and the vast area of Central Asia stretching from Turkey to Afghanistan. It was a vast area inhabited by the most backward people. They were predominantly Muslim by religion and their allegiance to the revolution was to be won without hurting their religious susceptibilities. He went to Tashkent where he was made a member of the Central Asiatic Bureau. He left for Tashkent with two train-loads of a variety of arms and a large treasure. The idea was to establish a base in Afghanistan and use the arms and the treasure to win over frontier tribes and through them establish contacts with revolutionary elements in India. But the plan had to be dropped owing to lack of cooperation from the Government of Afghanistan.

The arms and the military officers who accompanied them proved useful eventually for subduing the British inspired revolts and for imparting military training to Indian Muhajirs.

Roy studied the Quran and other religious books of Islam. While taking care not to hurt the religious sentiments of the people he began to justify the revolution on the ground of equality preached by Islam. That removed the misgivings of the people. The Emir and the Khan were eventually subdued through military operations and revolution was spread to Bokhara and Khiva. By that time, about 30-40,000 Indians had entered the area who were bent upon going to Turkey to fight for the Khilafat. Some of them were captured by Turkoman rebels and were grossly ill-treated. Roy sent a detachment of the Red Army for their rescue. After rescue, they were taken to Bokhara where Roy had talks with them. They were provided with military training. In October 1920, the Communist Party was also formed in Tashkent. Roy went to Moscow where he wrote an important book, *India in Transition*. It provides the first ever analysis of the Indian situation from the Marxist point of view. The book was also translated into Russian, German and many other languages. The book was sold well in Europe and the USA.

While in Russia or in Germany, Roy used to keep himself well informed of the happenings in India during the year. He never regarded the Congress Party as the political party of the bourgeoisie. To him, it was a mass movement of immense potentiality, but saddled with a reactionary leadership. He desired that leadership be thrown out and replaced by a revolutionary leadership. Early in 1927, the Comintern sent Roy to China as its representative to supervise the implementation of a new thesis that it had adopted. He played a major role in drafting the thesis that was adopted by ECCI at its meeting in Moscow in November 1926. The central point of the thesis was that the Chinese revolution must be thereafter developed as an agrarian revolution and that no fetish should be made of the alliance with the Kuomintang.

When Roy returned to India, he was a full-fledged communist. He had broken with the Comintern but not with communism. The old leaders of the party were in jail, involved in the Meerut Communist Conspiracy Case. The leadership was in the hands of a young inexperienced group. After his return to India, and for many years thereafter, the worst hostility that Roy had to face was from the CPI, the Comintern and its adherents. The CPI was not happy with Roy's return to India. When Roy returned, the Civil Disobedience Movement was already on the decline. The Roy Group tried to stop the decline through agitation and propaganda amongst Congressmen. It set up for this purpose organisations like Youth Leagues, Navjawan Bharat Sabhas and Independence of India Committees. In the end, the movement was withdrawn on the basis of the Gandhi-Irwin Pact.

In view of his revolutionary activities, Roy was arrested in Bombay (now Mumbai) on 21 July 1931 and was taken to Kanpur to stand trial for his part in the Kanpur Communist Conspiracy. He was sentenced for twelve years, which later on appeal, was reduced to six years' imprisonment. While in jail, he established contact with the outside world. He wrote a number of letters, articles, manifestoes and a book, *China in Revolt,* published under the pen name of S.K. Vidyarthi in 1935. *My Experiences in*

China and *Our Task in India* followed it. He was not allowed to make the defence statement, which was later published as *My Defence*. Some of his letters were published under the name, *Letters to the Congress Socialist Party*. Some of his articles were published in *The Mahratta* of Pune and *The Advocate* of Bombay. But, while in jail, he was never caught. Ordinarily, Roy was a well-behaved prisoner. Officially, he wrote only one letter a month to Ellen Gottschalk, who, after Roy's release, came to India, married him and made India her home. Roy found in Ellen Roy not only a loving wife but also an intelligent helper and close collaborator. They were published in 1941 as *Letters from Jail*. These letters provide a glimpse of Roy's wide knowledge and all-embracing interests. Life in jail shattered Roy's health. In 1934, he became so alarmingly ill that during summer months he was removed to Almora and brought back again to Bareilly after the summer was over. The next year, he was taken to Dehra Dun when the weather became hot and kept there until his release.

Roy suffered from dilation of heart and pain in the chest and slow fever from time to time. Many eminent persons, including the famous scientist, Albert Einstein, made representations to the Government of India and England for humane treatment to Roy. Jawaharlal Nehru also took personal interest in the matter, but to no avail. As an undertrial, he was an A-class prisoner but after conviction he was given B-class. But in spite of his ill-health Roy did plenty of writing in jail. He wrote about one thousand pages, which are strictly legal in nature. He was released from the Dehra Dun jail on 20 November 1936 after an imprisonment lasting five years and four months. The Congress leaders received him. In his first statement to the people he asked the countrymen to rally in millions under the flag of the National Congress as a determined army fighting for democratic freedom. He expressed his desire to formally enroll himself as a member of the Congress. On release, he brought with him the manuscript of a thousand pages prepared in the prison. It was published as books. *Fascism, Materialism, Historical Role of Islam, Ideals of Indian Womanhood* are the books that were made from those hand-written notebooks. A part of it was later published as *M.N. Roy Memoirs.*

Roy attended the Faizpur session of the Congress held in December 1936. Jawaharlal Nehru welcomed Roy into the fold of the Congress as a veteran fighter for freedom. In his speech, Roy outlined a concrete programme of action for involving the large masses in the national struggle by identifying it with the people's struggles for their immediate demands. The speech had a profound effect upon the audience. There he had his first face-to-face meeting with Mahatma Gandhi. In April 1937, he began the publication of his weekly journal, *Independent India,* to express his views on national and international developments. The Roy Group became more active after Roy's release. Its membership increased and it became a powerful factor in the political and the trade union field. Later, in the year, he toured Tamil Nadu and Andhra Pradesh. He went to Bengal, the land of his birth, where he was welcomed as a hero and was heard with rapt attention. He and his wife now settled down in Dehradun.

In 1940, Roy was elected President of the Congress. He delivered many lectures on Marxism and Communism and social revolution. He was the only leader to stress the necessity of a philosophical revolution. He did plenty of political writings. A number of his books were published. Prominent amongst them were: *Fascism, Historical Role of Islam, Our Problems* and *Letters to the CSP*. In September 1939, the Second World War started. The Congress began by resigning ministerial offices as a protest against the Viceroy's action involving India in the war without consulting the Central Legislative Assembly or the leaders of the people. It then moved on to the position of conditional co-operation. But the Viceroy and the British Government refused to fulfill the conditions and thus pushed the Congress in the direction of a struggle which culminated in the Quit India Movement in August 1942. Roy approved neither the course the Congress had adopted nor its attitude towards the war. He tried to persuade the Congress leaders not to adopt a hostile attitude towards the war. He prepared a thesis on the war which explained how it was not an imperialist but an internecine war which did not invite the application of the Leninist dictum of opposition to an imperialist war. The catastrophic developments in Europe had a profound effect on Roy. He proposed 14 July, the French Revolution Day, to the Congress for demonstrations all over the country to express sympathy and solidarity with France which had just been conquered by Hitler. The suggestion was turned down. Roy resigned from the Congress.

After discovering the faults and shortcomings of communism, in the last phase of his life, Roy moved away from communism and began his journey towards radical humanism. After the War, he re-examined many communist doctrines and theories. He was shocked and distressed when he found, at the end of the war, Stalin throwing away the moral leadership of progressive forces which was his, and trying to embark on a military conquest of Europe. He found in communism an utter disregard of and contempt for man, who had been reduced to the position of a helpless pawn in the hands of blind economic forces and an insignificant unit in the broad collectivity of a class. That happened also under capitalism. Neither capitalism nor communism showed the way out of the crisis. He thought of organised democracy and cooperative economy as a solution to the crisis which had gripped the world and was dragging it in the direction of war and destruction. He thought that both organised democracy and cooperative economy should have a philosophical foundation. Freedom is the basic value in radical humanism. As a philosophy of life, it covers the entire field of human existence from abstract thought to social and political reconstruction. It does not believe in transcendentalism. Roy explained that radical humanism had taken over the tradition of the founders of modern civilisation, the tradition of the revolt of man against the tyranny of God and his agents on this earth.

Roy was anxious to retire from politics, settle down in Dehradun and devote himself completely to reading and writing. In 1946, the RDP decided to contest elections to the provincial assemblies. Roy had to play a major role in guiding and organising the election campaign. He was anxious that transfer of power should be made to the people and not to political parties claiming to represent them. But he did not succeed in his mission. He wrote extensively on national and international affairs in his own journal, renamed *Radical Humanist*, in English and American journals. He now thought that revolution was a necessity but it was not possible to bring it about through the old method of armed insurrection owing to the tremendous military power of modern states. The new way, he thought, was through persuasion. His contributions to the discussions at Dehradun Camp are collected together in a book *New Orientation* published by the Renaissance Publishers of Calcutta. Radical Humanism brought Roy nearer to Mahatma Gandhi and his school of thought. Roy's own ideas about Mahatma Gandhi also underwent a big change in the last couple of years of the latter life. Roy realised that Mahatma Gandhi was a big moral force. He was shocked when he received news of Mahatma Gandhi's assassination.

Roy wrote more books, the most prominent of which is *Reason, Romanticism and Revolution*. Its first volume was published in 1953 and the second a year later after his death. It provides the quintessence of Roy's theoretical basis for the philosophy of radical humanism. Roy now needed rest and went to Mussoorie in June 1952 with his wife. While returning from his morning walk along a hill track he stumbled, fell and rolled down the hill about fifty feet below. He sustained grave injuries and had to be in bed for several weeks. When recovered, he was back to Dehradun and was thinking of resuming his work. By May 1953, he began to plan a visit to the United States for medical treatment and for fulfilling many engagements. But in August he had an attack of cerebral thrombosis. His illness became more and more serious. Ultimately, on 25 January 1954, a little before the beginning of Republic Day, he expired. Thus ended the untiring life of trials and tribulations and sustained struggle that was responsible for ushering independence to the country and a good deal of creative ideas to the progeny. M. N. Roy was a rare combination of a political activist, scholar and a thinker. The books he penned range from politics and economics to philosophy and natural sciences.